Teacher's Book 2
Ages 6 – 7

Marian Bond

Pearson Education Limited
Edinburgh Gate, Harlow, Essex CM20 2JE, England

© Pearson Education Limited 1999

The right of Marian Bond to be identified as the author of this Work has been asserted by her in accordance with the Copyright, Designs and Patents Act, 1988.

All rights reserved. No part of this publication may be reproduced, stored in a retrieval system, or transmitted in any form or by any means, electronic, mechanical, photocopying, recording, or otherwise without the prior written permission of the Publishers. This publication is not included under the licences issued by the Copyright Licensing Agency Ltd, 90 Tottenham Court Road, London W1P 9HE.

First published 1999

ISBN 0 582 42038 5

Printed in China

Series consultant: Penny Coltman

Designed by Ken Vail Graphic Design Ltd, Cambridge

Photography by Gareth Boden

The Publishers' policy is to use paper manufactured from sustainable forests.

Contents

		Page
Introduction		4
Links to the Framework for teaching mathematics		8
Unit 1	Counting	10
Unit 2	Place value 1	12
Unit 3	Place value 2	14
Unit 4	Number patterns 1	16
Unit 5	Ordering	18
Unit 6	Addition 1	20
Unit 7	Special numbers	22
Unit 8	Number bonds	24
Unit 9	Subtraction	26
Unit 10	Addition 2	28
Unit 11	Multiplication 1	30
Unit 12	Fractions	32
Unit 13	Number patterns 2	34
Unit 14	Addition 3	36
Unit 15	Multiplication 2	38
Unit 16	Division	40
Unit 17	Addition and subtraction	42
Unit 18	More number problems	44

Other areas of the curriculum:

Shape and space	46
Measure	47
Data handling	48

Introduction

Numeracy Big Board and whole class teaching

Numeracy Big Board has been designed to meet the needs of teachers addressing the National Numeracy Strategy and, in Scotland, the recommendations in Improving Mathematics 5–14. It is the ideal solution to the challenge of whole class teaching, incorporating both books and equipment.

During whole class activities the Big Board functions as a lively and stimulating focus. Opportunities should be planned for children to interact with the board. Repetitive handling and positioning of the numbers, shapes and pictures will not only be enjoyable, but will help to consolidate learning.

When introducing teaching points, the equipment, in conjunction with the activities described in the books, provides illustrations of number facts and properties. Developing familiarity with the resource will help children to feel confident as it is used to support new learning.

This book provides detailed suggestions about how to use Numeracy Big Board to teach the whole class. The book is organised by content area, so look at your planning each week and select in advance the activities you want to use to fit in with your work for the week.

Numeracy Big Board and other parts of the Maths lesson

Although Numeracy Big Board has been designed with the problem of whole class teaching firmly in mind, the equipment can be used in other parts of your Maths lessons as well.

Whole class mental maths activities can be carried out using the Board and equipment.

As children separate into groups for differentiated tasks, the Big Board can be moved around the room to provide the basis of an independent group activity, or to facilitate further teaching.

In plenary sessions, the Big Board provides a medium for the compilation of summative statements relating to the lesson. Its interactive aspects will also allow groups and individuals to present ideas and findings to the rest of the class.

Using the resources

The Big Board is provided with overlays which include the most commonly used templates and visual aids needed to teach numeracy. Other formats can be drawn, or recordings made, on the white magnetic surface or the overlays using a dry wipe (i.e. water-based, non-permanent) marker pen.

Important: Take care never to write on the Big Board or the overlays with permanent ink!

Although many useful activities can be carried out with the overlays and writing alone, they become a much more flexible and interactive tool when used in conjunction with the magnetic cards.

The cards are designed to be durable, but are best stored safely in a tray when not in use. Explain to the children that, like any other magnets, the cards should be handled carefully.

As well as a wide range of other resources, a selection of character cards are included: elephants, monkeys, children and object cards 1–20. These cards will provide contexts for counting or calculation and will also encourage children to develop the skills of imagery when working with number. The elephants are printed in four colours and three sizes, so that they additionally form a useful basis for sorting, logic and pattern-based activities.

The coloured squares and dots can be used as counters or markers. They can also be used as an infinite selection of imaginary items to provide contexts for numeracy problems. Enjoy some lateral thinking!

Using the books

The books provide a selection of activities which suggest how the Big Board can be used in teaching most aspects of Number. At the end of the book there is a section of ideas about how to extend your use of the equipment into the other areas of the Maths curriculum.

To help you plan your numeracy teaching, the books are divided into double-page spreads. Each spread contains activities designed to address a particular area of learning. They are intended to be used to support your existing scheme of work for Mathematics. Select activities as and when they are appropriate, in order to meet your particular needs.

The activities can be repeated and varied many times to practise and develop the learning objectives concerned.

Each activity has:

- a clearly defined learning objective

  These objectives are linked to specific targets in the development of numeracy.

- a list of resources needed

  Nearly all the resources listed will be part of the Big Board apparatus. The only exceptions are occasional pieces of standard classroom equipment, such as dice.

- preparation advice

  Sometimes it is helpful to have some cards in position on the Big Board at the beginning of the lesson. In other activities a drawn format or picture is required on the board.

- a description of the activity

  Familiarise yourself with this information before teaching the activity, in order to preserve spontaneity in your teaching.

  The information in this section includes:
  – a step-by-step guide to teaching the activity
  – opportunities to introduce interactive elements to the lesson
  – suggestions for productive questions.

In addition, many activities contain suggestions for extension.

Where appropriate, ideas are suggested for ways in which the Big Board apparatus can be further used to extend or challenge more able children.

Be creative!

This Teacher's Book will give you an invaluable starting point by providing a wealth of planned activities using Big Board. However, the list of activities described is only a beginning.

Big Board is intended to be enjoyable to use. As you become familiar with the equipment, explore its possibilities and enjoy supplementing the suggested activities with many more of your own ideas.

Links to the Framework for teaching mathematics

Unit 1: Counting
- Say the number names in order to at least 100, from and back to zero.
- Count on or back in ones or tens, starting from any two-digit number.
- Read and write whole numbers to at least 100 in figures and words.
- Order whole numbers to at least 100, and position them on a number line and 100 square.

Unit 2: Place value 1
- Count reliably up to 100 objects by grouping them: for example in tens, then fives or twos.
- Count on or back in ones or tens, starting from any two-digit number.
- Read and write whole numbers to at least 100 in figures and words.
- Know what each digit in a two-digit number represents, including 0 as a place holder, and partition two-digit numbers into a multiple of ten and ones (TU).

Unit 3: Place value 2
- Know what each digit in a two-digit number represents, including 0 as a place holder, and partition two-digit numbers into a multiple of ten and ones (TU).
- Compare two given two-digit numbers, say which is more or less, and give a number which lies between them.

Unit 4: Number patterns 1
- Count on or back in ones or tens, starting from any two-digit number.
- Count on in twos from and back to zero or any small number.
- Recognise odd and even numbers to at least 30.
- Count on in steps of 3, 4 or 5 to at least 30, from and back to zero, then from and back to any given small number.
- Compare two given two-digit numbers, say which is more or less, and give a number which lies between them.

Unit 5: Ordering
- Use and begin to read the vocabulary of comparing and ordering numbers, including ordinal numbers to 100.
- Compare two given two-digit numbers, say which is more or less, and give a number which lies between them.
- Order whole numbers to at least 100, and position them on a number line and 100 square.

Unit 6: Addition 1
- Say the number that is 1 or 10 more or less than any given two-digit number.
- Use the +, − and = signs to record mental additions and subtractions in a number sentence, and recognise the use of a symbol to stand for an unknown number.
- Use knowledge that addition can be done in any order to do mental calculations more efficiently.
- Add/subtract 9 or 11: add/subtract 10 and adjust by 1.

Unit 7: Special numbers
- Know by heart doubles of all numbers to 10 and the corresponding halves.
- Derive quickly doubles of multiples of 5 to 50.

Unit 8: Number bonds
- Know by heart all addition and subtraction facts for each number to at least 10.
- Know by heart all pairs of numbers with a total of 20.
- Use patterns of similar calculations.
- Use known number facts and place value to add/subtract mentally.

Unit 9: Subtraction
- Understand that subtraction is the inverse of addition (subtraction reverses addition).
- Know by heart all addition and subtraction facts for each number to at least 10.
- Know by heart all pairs of numbers with a total of 20.
- Find a small difference by counting up from the smaller to the larger number.
- Use patterns of similar calculations.

Unit 10: Addition 2
- Use knowledge that addition can be done in any order to do mental calculations more efficiently. For example: put the larger number first and count on in tens and ones; add three small numbers by putting the largest number first and/or find a pair totalling 10; partition into '5 and a bit' when adding 6, 7, 8 or 9, then recombine.
- Use patterns of similar calculations.
- Bridge through 10 or 20, then adjust.

Unit 11: Multiplication 1
- Understand the operation of multiplication as repeated addition or as describing an array, and begin to understand division as grouping (repeated subtraction) or sharing.
- Know by heart multiplication facts up to 5×5.

Unit 12: Fractions
- Begin to recognise and find one half and one quarter of shapes and small numbers of objects.
- Begin to recognise that two halves or four quarters make one whole and that two quarters and one half are equivalent.

Unit 13: Number patterns 2
- Count on in steps of 3, 4 or 5 to at least 30, from and back to zero, then from and back to any given small number.
- Begin to recognise two-digit multiples of 2, 5 or 10.
- Recognise simple patterns and relationships, generalise and predict.

Unit 14: Addition 3
- Count reliably up to 100 objects by grouping them: for example in tens, then fives or twos.
- Understand that more than two numbers can be added.
- Begin to add three single-digit numbers mentally (totals up to about 20) or three two-digit numbers with the help of apparatus (totals up to 100).
- Use knowledge that addition can be done in any order to do mental calculations more efficiently. For example: put the larger number first and count on in tens and ones; add three small numbers by putting the largest number first and/or find a pair totalling 10; partition into '5 and a bit' when adding 6, 7, 8 or 9, then recombine; partition additions into tens and units, then recombine.

Unit 15: Multiplication 2
- Begin to recognise two-digit multiples of 2, 5 or 10.
- Know by heart: multiplication facts for the 2 and 10 times-tables; multiplication facts up to 5×5. Begin to know multiplication facts for the 5 times-table.

Unit 16: Division
- Understand the operation of multiplication as repeated addition or as describing an array, and begin to understand division as grouping (repeated subtraction) or sharing.
- Use known number facts and place value to carry out mentally simple multiplications and divisions.

Unit 17: Addition and subtraction
- Count on or back in ones or tens, starting from any two-digit number.
- Count on in twos from and back to zero or any small number.
- Count on in steps of 3, 4 or 5 to at least 30, from and back to zero, then from and back to any given small number.
- Use known number facts and place value to add/subtract mentally.
- Derive quickly doubles of all numbers to at least 15.

Unit 18: More number problems
- Use and begin to read the vocabulary of estimation and approximation; give a sensible estimate of at least 50 objects.
- Round numbers less than 100 to the nearest 10.
- Use mental addition and subtraction, simple multiplication and division, to solve simple word problems involving numbers in 'real life', money or measures, using one or two steps. Explain how the problem was solved.

Unit 1: Counting

① Counting sheep

Learning objective	To consolidate the names of numbers greater than 10. (It is based on the true origin of the words 'eleven' and 'twelve'.)
Resources	• 15–20 assorted coloured squares • word cards for 'nine' to 'twelve' • optional: word cards for 'thirteen' to 'ninety'
Preparation	Draw a ring on the board which will take exactly ten coloured squares or 'sheep'.

This story is about a man who lived in Anglo-Saxon England. He kept sheep and every night he put them in a pen for safe-keeping. Each night he counted his sheep as they went into the pen.

▶ Count nine sheep into the pen. Put the word 'nine' on the board.

One day he went to the market and bought a sheep. That night he counted his sheep into the pen.

▶ Count ten sheep into the pen. Put the word 'ten' on the board.

Some time later he went to the market again and bought another sheep. That night he counted his sheep into the pen.

▶ Count ten sheep into the pen and have one left over.

He ran to his wife and shouted, 'Wife, Wife, we have ten sheep and one left over! What shall we do?' His wife tells him to build another pen.

▶ Draw another ring, the same size as the first and put the spare sheep in it.

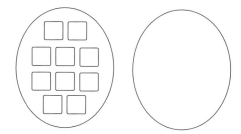

▶ Repeat the counting '… ten, one left over' a couple of times.
Explain that the men gets fed up with such a long mouthful and shortens it to 'eleven'.

▶ Put the word *eleven* on the board.

▶ Remove the sheep from the board and put twelve sheep in your hand.

His cousin in the next village also keeps sheep. He counts them into the pen.

▶ Count ten into the pen and have two left over.

He says he has 'ten and two left over'.

▶ Count them into the pen again 'one, two, … ten, one-left-over-, two-left-over'. Ask what 'two-left-over' gets shortened to. Put the word *twelve* on the board.

Extension

▶ Develop the story to count 'three and ten', 'four and ten', and so on to 'ten and ten' which is changed to 'two-tens' and on to 'three-tens', and so on to 'nine-tens'.

② What's my name?

Learning objective	To be able to read the number names to 20.
Resources	• number word cards • picture cards 1–20
Preparation	This game should be adapted according to the capabilities of the children. The first time it is played place the number word cards in order on the left-hand half of the board. On the other half of the board randomly spread the picture cards (start with 1–5).

▶ Ask one child at a time to choose a picture card and put it next to the correct number word card.

▶ When all the picture cards are used up, replace them on the right-hand side and continue the game until every child has had a turn. Alternatively, place the picture cards in order and mix up the words. As a third variation, place both the word and picture cards randomly on the board.

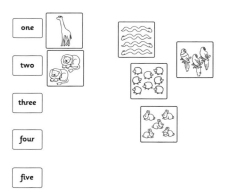

Extension

▶ Repeat the activity but use the number cards instead of the picture cards.

Unit 1: Counting

③ Next please!

Learning objective	To be able to say the number names in order (and reverse order) to 100.
Resources	• 100 square overlay

▶ As a class, read the numbers from 1–20 as you point to each number in turn on the 100 square overlay. Choose any other 'two decades', e.g. 51–70, and read these numbers. Repeat the activity, counting backwards, e.g. 80–61. When you count backwards from 20, remind the children that *zero* means *none* or *not any*.

▶ When the children are ready, repeat the activity without pointing at the board.

▶ Divide the class into groups of about six. For each group, give a starting number, e.g. 24. Each child in turn has to say the next number. Give the next group a new starting number. If a child cannot provide the next number refer to the 100 square overlay and let them see which number comes next.

▶ When each group has had a turn at *counting forwards* ask them to *count backwards* from a number you give them.

④ Bingo!

Learning objective	To be able to identify where any two-digit number fits on the 100 square overlay.
Resources	• 10 × 10 grid overlay • number cards 1–100 • drawstring bag
Preparation	Until the children are familiar with the 100 square overlay you may wish to place a few cards on the grid before you start (e.g. 1, 11, 21, ... 91).

▶ The object of the game is to fill the blank 10 × 10 grid with numbers. The game becomes easier as more cards are placed on the grid. Put the number cards in the bag. Ask a child to take one and put it in the correct place on the grid.

▶ At first the children may have to count from the 1 square to find the correct place. When the children are familiar with the pattern of the numbers on the 100 square overlay they will be able to find the correct square more efficiently by counting along to find the correct *unit column* and down to find the correct *tens row*. For example, 26 is 6 along to find 6 and then 3 rows down to find 26.

▶ Encourage the children to think of the quickest way to place their number. It may be by counting on or back in ones from a number already on the grid, or it may be by counting up or down in tens, or a combination of both.

⑤ Reach 100

Learning objective	To be able to count on from any number up to 100.
Resources	• 100 square overlay • one marker dot • digit cards 1–6 • drawstring bag • optional: coloured square cards

▶ Put the dot where zero would be, to the left of the one, on the 100 square overlay. Ask one child to pick a card from the bag and say the number out loud. The child moves the marker dot to the appropriate number on the 100 square overlay.

▶ Remind the children that the 100 square overlay doesn't zig-zag like a 'Snakes and Ladders' board. When they reach the end of one row they must go to the beginning of the next. The other children should think about where they would put the counter. Check if they all agree.

▶ Put the number back in the bag and ask another child to draw a card. They say the number out loud and move the marker dot to the appropriate square (by counting on). Again check if the other children agree or disagree. Continue the game until you reach 100.

1	2	3	4	5	6	7		9	10
11	12	13	14	15	16	17	18	19	20
21		23	24	25	26	27	○		30
31	32	33		35	36	37	38	39	40
41	42	43	44	45	46	47	48	49	50
51	52	53	54	55	56	57	58	59	60
61	62	63	64	65	66	67	68	69	70
71		73	74	75	76	77	78	79	80
81	82	83	84	85	86	87	88	89	
91	92	93	94		96	97	98	99	100

Note: Dice could be used instead of digit cards inside a drawstring bag.

Extension

▶ Cover some of the numbers with a coloured square. If the counter lands on a covered square there is a penalty or bonus. Choose what happens according to the capabilities of your children. For example:
– the counter has to move on or back by one, two or three squares (you choose)
– the counter has to move up or down by one row (remind the children this is counting on or back by ten)
– the child has to answer a simple mathematical question about the hidden number.

Unit 2: Place value 1

1 Dotty groups

Learning objective	To understand the connection between grouping objects in tens and the way we write numbers.
Resources	• marker dots of assorted colours
Preparation	Place about 27 dots at random on the board.

How many dots are there on the board?

▶ Tell the children not to count the dots, but to *estimate* how many. Try counting the dots to check their estimates, but go wrong and 'forget' which you have counted and which you have not.

How could we make the counting easier?

▶ You want the children to suggest *grouping* the dots. They may suggest arranging the dots in groups of two or five or perhaps three or four. Group the dots as they suggest, separating the left-over dots from the rest. Make each group a recognisable pattern as this provides a quick way to check you have the correct number in each group, and gives the children a visual image of each number.

▶ Now count the dots by multiple addition. They may find grouping in two or five is useful if they are familiar with counting in 2s or 5s. End up by grouping in tens.

▶ Write the number of dots next to the pattern you have made. Keep the results on the board and repeat the activity for two or three more numbers of dots.

Look at the groups of dots and at the numbers. What do you notice?

▶ You want the children to see that the *first digit* in the number is the same as the number of groups of ten, and the *last digit* is the same as the number of left-over dots. Write 18 on the board.

What groups will we end up with if I put 18 dots on the board?

▶ If necessary, demonstrate that you get one group of ten and eight left over. Remove the dots and repeat with other two-digit numbers (all digits greater than zero) until all the children understand the connection between the groups and the number.

What groups will we get if I put 20 dots on the board?

▶ Arrange the 20 dots and write *2* (for two whole groups of ten) on the board.

▶ Ask the children if they agree with what you have written. You want the children to tell you that *2* means *two* dots, but you want to say *twenty* dots. You need to write *2* whole groups and *0* left over, i.e. 20. Check that they understand by asking about 40, 70, etc.

2 Tens and units

Learning objective	To be able to explain what digits in tens and units columns mean.
Resources	• number line overlay • number cards 35–45 • 2 sets of digit cards 0–9
Preparation	Draw in tens and units columns under the number line. Set out the number cards 35–45 on the number line.

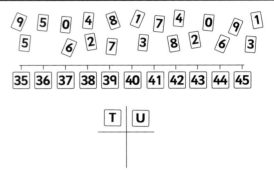

Look at the number line. What numbers do we have?

▶ Read the numbers.

What do the numbers mean? What does thirty-eight mean?

▶ Possible answers are:

If you had 38 sweets and 38 people they could have one each.

The 3 means three tens and the 8 means eight units. The first number tells us how many tens there are and the second number tell us how many units or single things there are.

▶ Spread the two sets of digit cards 0–9 at random at the top of the board. As you talk about 38 put an 8 in the *units column* and a 3 in the *tens column*. Ask a child to describe 42 (i.e. 4 tens and 2 units) and put the correct digits in the correct columns. Check that all the children agree.

▶ When you think all the children can correctly identify the tens and units for the numbers on the number line, ask them about numbers they cannot see, e.g. 84, 16, 50, 7, etc.

Unit 2: Place value 1

③ Name a number

Learning objective	To be able to name and write in figures any two-digit number.
Resources	• 2 sets of digit cards 0–9 • marker dots in two colours • drawstring bag
Preparation	Divide the class into two teams and draw a scoreboard for the teams on the board.

▶ Place the cards in the bag and draw out two of them. Put them on the board in the order they were drawn to make a two-digit number. (Discuss what to do if a zero is drawn first – ignore it.) Ask a child in team 1 to read the number. If they get it wrong ask a member of team 2. The team which answers correctly gets a point in the form of a marker dot.

▶ Replace the digits and repeat the activity asking team 2 first.

▶ As a variation you could put four sets of digits on the board. Ask one member of each team to come to the board. You say a two-digit number, including the 'teens'. The first child to make the number correctly with the digit cards wins the point.

Extension

▶ Play the game again but take three cards or name three-digit numbers.

④ Counting in ones and tens

Learning objective	To be able to count on or back in ones or tens by increasing/decreasing the appropriate digit by one.
Resources	• 10 x 10 grid • 100 square overlay
Preparation	Fill in the grid as a 100 number square, but write the figures in columns instead of rows, ensuring that all the tens and units align.

1	11	21	31	41	51	61	71	81	91
2	12	22	32	42	52	62	72	82	92
3	13	23	33	43	53	63	73	83	93
4	14	24	34	44	54	64	74	84	94
5	15	25	35	45	55	65	75	85	95
6	16	26	36	46	56	66	76	86	96
7	17	27	37	47	57	67	77	87	97
8	18	28	38	48	58	68	78	88	98
9	19	29	39	49	59	69	79	89	99
10	20	30	40	50	60	70	80	90	100

▶ Explain that you have arranged the numbers differently from the way the children are used to, going down instead of across. As a class, read the numbers 1–10, pointing at them as you do so. Now count 41–50 as a class.

When we count, what are we counting on by? What are we adding to each number? (One)

What happens to the number in the units column as we count? (It increases by one.)

What happens to the number in the tens column as we count? (It stays the same.)

▶ These two statements are true most of the time, but when we reach a nine in the units column the tens go up by one and the units go back to zero.

▶ Repeat the activity but this time count backwards. Ask the same questions.

▶ Replace the grid with the 100 square overlay. (You could use the grid you have drawn, but it is easier to see the changing digit if you are comparing numbers written in a vertical list.) As a class, count in tens from 10–100 pointing at the numbers as you do so. Now count in tens from 6 to 96 as a class.

What were we counting on by this time? What are adding to each number? (Ten)

What happens to the number in the tens column as we count in tens? (It increases by one.)

What happens to the number in the units column as we count in tens? (It stays the same.)

▶ Explain that when we reach a nine in the tens column, we put a 1 in the next column (hundreds) and set the tens back to zero.

▶ Repeat the activity but this time count backwards. Ask the same questions.

▶ Ask the children to give you numbers one/ten more/less than any number on the 100 square overlay. Include zero and up to one hundred and nine for answers, but no negative numbers.

Unit 3: Place value 2

1) What's it worth?

Learning objective	To identify a two-digit number by tens and units.
Resources	• 20 marker dots in two colours • drawstring bag
Preparation	Draw tens and units columns on the board. You may wish to label another set of tens and units columns so the dots can be sorted into columns as they are drawn from the bag.

▶ On the board write:

● = 10 (ten)   ○ = 1 (unit)

▶ Put the remaining 18 dots in the bag and remove four of them. Ensure you have some of each colour.

● ○ ○ ●

▶ Ask a child to arrange the dots so the tens are on the left and the units are on the right.

What number do these dots represent? How much do they mean? **(Two tens and two units: 22)**

▶ Write *22* in the tens and unit columns. Put the dots back and ask a child to draw out six dots. Ask another child to arrange the dots and ask the whole class what they represent.

▶ Repeat the activity with each child drawing out up to nine dots. Discuss carefully what the dots mean if only tens or only units are drawn out.

2) Who has more?

Learning objective	To understand the value of digits according to their place in a number.
Resources	• sets of digit cards 0–9 (2 sets gives 9 goes, 3 sets gives 14 goes, 6 sets gives 29 goes) • drawstring bag
Preparation	Divide the board into two halves with a vertical line. You could split the class into two teams but it is not essential to have winners.

▶ Put all the digit cards into the bag and take out two, ensuring they are different, e.g. 2 and 6. Hold the cards up for the class to see.

If I write these two digits down, what numbers could I make? **(26 and 62)**

▶ Write *26* and *62* on the board.

Which is larger? Why?

▶ Return the cards to the bag and ask two children to take two cards each from the bag. They must place them on their half of the board so that they make the largest number they can. Check that the other children agree with their decision. For example, if Bill picks 1 and 7 and Ben picks 2 and 4, Bill would make 71 and Ben would make 42. When a child picks a zero, discuss how it may mean no units or no tens. Explain that 04 means the same as 4. We don't need put the tens if there are none in a two-digit number.

Who has made the larger number, Bill or Ben? **(Bill wins this round.)**

A	B
7 1	4 2

▶ The larger number stays on the board and the other two cards are returned to the bag. Ask two more children to make a two-digit number. Keep the larger number on the board as before and return the other two cards to the bag. Continue until there are only two cards left.

▶ Look at the numbers that are left on the board.

A	B
7 1	6 3
5 0	8 4
6 2	9 5
7 2	8 3
	4 1

Which is the largest number on the board? **(That team wins.)**

Extension

▶ Play in exactly the same way but aim to make the *lowest* number.

Unit 3: Place value 2

③ Pre-packed tens

Learning objective	To begin to understand how exchanging works.
Resources	• marker dots in two different colours • number cards 8, 11–19 • drawstring bag
Preparation	Draw tens and unit columns on the right-hand side of the board. Put the number card 8 on the board and the remaining cards in the bag. Separate the dots into two groups, one group of each colour.

▶ Ask a child to count out as many dots of one colour as are needed to represent eight and place them on the board. Arrange them in an easily countable pattern, e.g. two sets of four. Write the number *8* in the units column.

▶ Ask another child to pick a number from the bag and count out the appropriate number of dots (e.g. 16). Write the number on the board but put *16* in the units column. Ask if the children agree. Explain that we write only one digit in each column. It is true, you *do* have 16 units (16 dots) but we cannot write two digits in the units column.

What shall we do?

▶ Explain that we write the 1 in the next column, the tens column.

What do the digits mean? (One ten and six units)

▶ Show the children a marker dot of the second colour. Explain it is worth ten of the others – it is a 'pre-packed ten'. At the top of the board, put:

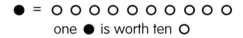

● = ○ ○ ○ ○ ○ ○ ○ ○ ○ ○
one ● is worth ten ○

▶ Look at the sixteen dots again. Ask a child to make the *exchange*. Compare the dots with the number 16 (i.e. one ten and six units in both cases).

● ○ ○ ○ ○ ○ ○

▶ Choose another number from the bag and repeat the activity, carrying out the exchange.

Extension

▶ Put number cards 1–99 in the bag. Ask a child to draw a number from the bag, represent it with tens and unit dots straightaway (i.e. don't count out 57 units and then exchange for five tens!) and write the digits in the appropriate columns.

④ My elephant says

Learning objective	To be able to place and name a number in H, T and U columns.
Resources	• 1 set of elephant cards • 2 sets of digit cards 0–9 • number cards 1, 10, 100 • drawstring bag
Preparation	Draw H, T and U columns on the board. Write H, T and U, and 100, 10 and 1 at the top of the appropriate columns. Put the number cards in the bag and place the elephant cards in a pile face down on the table.

▶ Draw a digit card from the bag (e.g. 6).

I have a six.

▶ Take the elephant card from the top of the pile.

My elephant says '100' (if it is large, '10' if it is medium-sized and '1' if it is small).

That makes 600.

▶ Write 600 in the columns. Return the number card to the bag and place the elephant card to one side. Ask the children in turn to pick a number and an elephant card and to say out loud what the elephant has changed the number into. Then get them to write the number on the board, combining with other numbers if possible, and to say the new number out loud. If the following cards are picked the board should look as shown.

card		H	T	U
		100	10	1
6	🐘			
2	🐘	6	2	1
1	🐘	3	8	0
8	🐘	9	0	0
3	🐘			
9	🐘			

▶ The children say, '600', '620', '621', '80', '380', '900'.

Unit 4: Number patterns 1

① Counting in tens

Learning objective	To be able to count on or back in multiples of ten.
Resources	• monkey cards • elephant cards • 100 square overlay • number cards 10, 20, 30, 40, 50, 60, 70, 80, 90, 100

▶ Count, or ask a child to count out ten monkeys. Arrange them in a line on the board and place the number card 10 next to them. Ask another child to count out ten more monkeys.

How many rows of monkeys are there? **(2)**
How many monkeys do we have now? **(20)**

▶ Put number card 20 next to the end of the second row.

▶ Continue *counting sets of ten* (now using the elephant cards) and keep a running total at the end of each set. When you have 40 animals on the board replace the cards with the 100 square overlay but keep the number cards and place them on the appropriate squares.

1	2	3	4	5	6	7	8	9	**10**
11	12	13	14	15	16	17	18	19	**20**
21	22	23	24	25	26	27	28	29	**30**
31	32	33	34	35	36	37	38	39	**40**
41	42	43	44	45	46	47	48	49	50
51	52	53	54	55	56	57	58	59	60
61	62	63	64	65	66	67	68	69	70
71	72	73	74	75	76	77	78	79	80
81	82	83	84	85	86	87	88	89	90
91	92	93	94	95	96	97	98	99	100

▶ Continue *counting in tens* and covering the square you land on up to 100. As a class, read aloud the squares you have covered.

What do you notice?

▶ You want the children to notice that all the numbers covered end with a *zero*. They will also notice the numbers form a column on the number square. Check that the children understand that each number covered is ten greater than the previous one.

What is ten more than 50, …70, …10, … etc.?

▶ Now read the covered numbers in reverse order. Ask what is ten fewer than 30, … 90, … 10, … etc.

② Counting in fives

Learning objective	To be able to count on or back in fives from any multiple of five up to 100.
Resources	• monkey and elephant cards • 100 square overlay • number cards 5, 10, 15, 20, … 100

▶ Approach this in the same way as the previous activity, but this time count out sets of five animals. When you have thirty animals on the board replace the cards with the 100 square overlay and cover the numbers you have already used. Continue *counting in fives* and covering the square you land on, up to 100. As a class, read aloud the squares you have covered. Read and move your hand in a rhythmical way to emphasise the pattern.

What do you notice?

▶ You want the children to notice that all the numbers covered end with a five or a zero. They will also notice the numbers form two columns on the number square. Check that the children understand that each number covered is five greater than the previous one.

What is five more than 5, 30, 65, … etc?

▶ Now read the covered numbers in reverse order. Ask what is five fewer than 45, 80, 5, … etc.

Note: Marker dots could be used instead of number cards.

③ Counting in twos

Learning objective	To be able to count on or back by two from any multiple of two less than 100.
Resources	• monkey cards • 100 square overlay • number cards 2, 4, 6, 8… 100

▶ Arrange the monkeys in *pairs*. Keep a running total of the number of monkeys, by placing the number cards 2, 4, 6, etc. next to each pair. When you have twenty monkeys on the board replace the cards with the 100 square overlay and cover the numbers you have already used. Continue *counting in twos* and covering the square you land on, up to 100. As a class, read aloud the squares you have covered.

What do you notice?

Unit 4: Number patterns 1

▶ The children should notice that all the numbers covered end with a two, four, six, eight or a zero. They will also notice the numbers form columns on the number square. Check the children understand that each number covered is two greater than the previous one.

What is two more than 6, 14, 50, ... etc?

▶ Now read a portion of the covered numbers in reverse order (e.g. 48–30). Ask what is two fewer than 48, 36, 88, 2, ... etc.

Note: Marker dots could be used instead of number cards.

1	2	3	4	5	6	7	8	9	10
11	12	13	14	15	16	17	18	19	20
21	22	23	24	25	26	27	28	29	30
31	32	33	34	35	36	37	38	39	40
41	42	43	44	45	46	47	48	49	50
51	52	53	54	55	56	57	58	59	60
61	62	63	64	65	66	67	68	69	70
71	72	73	74	75	76	77	78	79	80
81	82	83	84	85	86	87	88	89	90
91	92	93	94	95	96	97	98	99	100

▶ Start at two and, as a class, read aloud a portion of the covered numbers, e.g. 2–30. (You could start at one and clap on the odd numbers and say the even numbers.)

How many to the next number?
What were we counting in?
What do you notice about the numbers we have covered?

▶ You want the children to notice the repeating last digits of the numbers 2, 4, 6, 8 and 0. Teach the children the chant:

Two, four, six, eight,
Who do we appreciate?
C...L...A...S...S...2
Class 2!
(or any appropriate name)

▶ Ask if the children know what we call the numbers that have been covered. Explain they are called *even numbers*. Tell them the rhyme will help them remember the even numbers. Ask which digit is missing from the rhyme.

▶ Ask if the children know what we call the numbers that have not been covered. Explain they are called *odd numbers*. Point out they are the numbers which are not even. Say the odd numbers aloud by reading the 100 square overlay, this time clapping on the even numbers.

▶ Look at the number square and get the children to tell you if a number is even or odd. Ask them why they gave their answer (because of the digit it ends with).

Note: Marker dots could be used instead of number cards.

Extension

▶ Look at the numbers that are not covered. Ask the children what they notice about these numbers. They should spot the repeating end *digits* of 1, 3, 5, 7 and 9. Ask the children to tell you the numbers which are two larger or smaller than any of the odd numbers. (You could mention the words *even* and *odd* if you wish, but this will be covered in the next activity.)

4 Every other one

Learning objective	To identify the odd and even numbers.
Resources	• 100 square overlay • number cards 1–100

▶ Start by pointing where zero would be and read every other number. Cover each number as you land on it with the appropriate number card.

17

Unit 5: Ordering

① Getting bigger

Learning objective	To understand that higher numbers represent more objects than lower numbers.
Resources	• picture cards

▶ Show the children the 5 rabbits card and the 13 eggs card.

Which card has more objects on it? (Eggs – 13)

▶ Ask them to tell you how many objects each card represents (either from memory or by counting – you could ask them to estimate the numbers first). Write the numbers on the board next to the picture cards.

Which is the bigger number? Which number means 'more things'?

▶ Ask the children to compare other pairs of picture cards and to tell you the larger number.

② All in order

Learning objective	To learn that numbers can be arranged in an increasing or decreasing order. To learn vocabulary relating to order.
Resources	• number cards 1–100
Preparation	Sort the cards into groups of consecutive numbers: e.g. 1–10, 11–20, 35–44, 46–55, 58—67, 69–78, 82—91. Put the cards 1–10 on the board in a straight line but not in numerical order.

▶ As a class rearrange the cards to put them in the correct *counting order*. Use words such as *first, next, second, last,* etc. Repeat the exercise with 11–20. Ask a child to do the same thing with the cards 35–44. Continue until you are satisfied all the children could arrange any of the cards in consecutive numerical order.

▶ Take any of the sets of cards and arrange them in decreasing numerical order.

Is that all right?
What have I done?

▶ Explain that the cards are in order, but this time the numbers are *getting smaller* – you are counting backwards.

▶ Ask a child to arrange a set of the cards in *descending order*. Ask the other children if they agree with the arrangement. Repeat the exercise asking for some sets of cards to be arranged in *ascending order* and some in descending order.

③ Order those present

Learning objective	To be able to put any set of two-digit numbers in ascending or descending order.
Resources	• number cards 1–100 • drawstring bag
Preparation	Put the number cards in the bag.

▶ Take five or six cards from the bag and place them at random on the board. As a class, arrange them in ascending order.

▶ Replace the cards in the bag and place another set at random on the board. Ask a child to arrange these in descending order. Check that all the children agree.

▶ Repeat the activity until you are satisfied the children could arrange any given set of numbers in increasing or decreasing order.

Unit 5: Ordering

④ In between

Learning objective	To be able to provide a number between any two given two-digit numbers.
Resources	• number cards 1–100 • drawstring bag • optional: 100 square overlay

▶ Draw two cards from the bag and place them on the board. Put them on the number square if it is being used. Ask the children for any number *between* the numbers you picked. (Their answers must be strictly between and not include the picked numbers.) Explain that there may be more than one right answer.

▶ As the children's knowledge increases you could ask:

Give me a number which ends with 6 and which lies between the two numbers.

Give me any even/odd number between the two numbers.

Give me a number that we get when we count in fives and which lies between the two numbers.

Extension

▶ As the children's ability increases try the activity without using the number square as a reference.

⑤ Elephant train

Learning objective	To learn the names and meanings of the first ten ordinals.
Resources	• 10 elephant cards: large and small only, assorted colours • ordinal number cards 1st–10th
Preparation	Place five elephants on the board as if they are walking trunk to tail. Put a large (female) at the front and have a mixture of adults and babies following behind. The children might like to give each elephant a name.

▶ Explain that elephants walk in trains like this, with the baby elephants holding on to the tail of the elephant in front.

▶ Put the first five *ordinal number* cards at random on the board. Ask the children to put them in order above the elephants. Ask questions about the elephant train.

What colour is the first elephant?
Is the fifth elephant an adult or a baby?
Which position is the blue elephant in?

▶ Extend the train with five more elephants and place the ordinals 6th–10th above them. Ask more questions about the elephant train.

Extension 1

▶ Try asking questions without the ordinal number cards labelling the elephants.

Extension 2

▶ Ask more involved questions such as:

What colour is the elephant after the fourth elephant?
What positions are the red elephants in?
Is there a baby elephant next to the seventh elephant?

⑥ Calendars

Learning objective	To be able to name any ordinal up to thirty-first.
Resources	• number cards 1–31
Preparation	Set up the board and numbers as a calendar for the current month. Name the month and the days of the week. Make sure the children can also see today's date written out in full.

▶ Talk about the way we write the date.

Why is today called the xth?

▶ Look at the position of today on the calendar. Ask questions about the days.

MARCH				
Sunday		5	12	19	26
Monday		6	13	20	27
Tuesday		7	14	21	28
Wednesday	1	8	15	22	29
Thursday	2	9	16	23	30
Friday	3	10	17	24	31
Saturday	4	11	18	25	

What day of the week was the first of the month?
What day of the week is the last day of the month?
What will the date be on the last day of the month? (thirtieth, thirty-first, etc.)
What is the date of the first Saturday?
What is the date of the third Wednesday?
What is the date of the second Monday?

Extension

▶ Ask more complex questions:

What is the date on the day before the second Friday?
What is the day two days after the fourteenth?

Unit 6: Addition 1

1 Conservation of number

Learning objective	To ensure all children have grasped the concept of conservation of number.
Resources	• 15 monkey cards
Preparation	Draw a picture of two palm trees and the ground. Put all the monkeys in one of the trees.

▶ Before embarking on formal learning of addition children need to be aware that moving a set of objects does not alter its number.

How many monkeys are there? (15)

▶ With the children able to see what you are doing move some of the monkeys to the other tree or on to the ground.

How many monkeys are there?

▶ Every child should be able to answer immediately, without re-counting the monkeys. Repeat.

▶ Ask the children how they can be so sure about the number. None have been added, none have been taken away – they have just moved.

2 Matching

Learning objective	To ensure all children are able to count a set of objects by matching them to another set of objects of known size.
Resources	• 7 elephant cards • 7 face cards

▶ Put seven faces at random on the board.

How many faces are there?

▶ Obscure the board so that the children cannot see what you are doing and don't have the opportunity to count. Place an elephant immediately next to each face card.

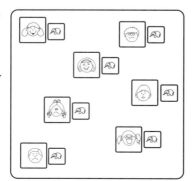

I have put some elephants on the board. How many are there?

▶ Show them the board. Every child should be able to answer immediately, without counting. Ask the children to explain how they 'knew' the answer. (You *matched* an elephant to a face. There were seven faces, so there must be seven elephants.) Repeat the activity using different numbers of elephants and face cards until you are satisfied every child could count a set by matching it with another set of a known number.

3 Counting on

Learning objective	To be able to count a total by counting on from a previously known total.
Resources	• addition/subtraction template overlay • marker dots in two colours • number cards 1–20 • word cards 'one' to 'twenty' • addition sign card • equals sign card

▶ Using one colour, put eight dots in the first ring.

How many dots?

▶ Place the word card 'eight' beneath the ring. Using the other colour, put six dots in the second ring.

How many dots?

▶ Place the word card 'six' beneath the second ring. Move the dots to the bottom ring.

How many dots altogether? How many dots are there on the board?

▶ Let the children answer (by counting them all if they wish) and put the word card 'fourteen' under the ring.

▶ Put the dots back in their original rings and check the children have the correct number by saying:

We had eight dots in this ring and then six more. Eight, (point to the first set) put eight in your head ... (point to your head) ... nine ... ten ... eleven ... twelve ... thirteen ... fourteen. (Point to each dot in the second ring as you count it.) There are fourteen altogether. We say we have added six to eight to get fourteen. Eight add six equals fourteen.

▶ Add the word cards 'add' and 'equals' to the words on the board and make the addition sentence.

▶ Explain that we can write the sentence in *numbers* and *symbols*. Make up the *number sentence*: 8 + 6 = 14 beneath the word sentence with the

Unit 6: Addition 1

numbers and symbols placed directly beneath the appropriate words.

▶ Repeat the activity, this time letting the children put the appropriate words and then the symbols on the board. (Keep the totals below twenty.) Each time demonstrate that addition can be done by counting on and that there is no need to recount the first set. Progress so that the children do not need/want to count out the dots for the first set. Make all the additions you do have the larger number first.

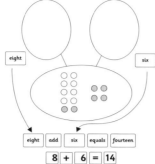

④ Add one

Learning objective	To be able to add one to any two-digit number.
Resources	• 100 square overlay • elephant cards • marker dots • number cards 1–100 • drawstring bag
Preparation	Choose a single-digit number. Place the number on the overlay. Put the remaining single-digit numbers in the bag.

▶ Ask each child to put the correct number of elephant cards on the board covering the number.

How many elephants will there be if I add one more elephant? What is one more than x?

▶ Add the extra elephant and count on to find the new number. Mark the new number on the board with a dot. Show the children that 'adding one' is the same as 'counting on one' or 'moving forward one' on the 100 square overlay.

▶ Choose another number from the bag and repeat the activity.

▶ After a few times put all the numbers in the bag and add one to the chosen number without using the elephants or number square as a reference.

Extension

▶ Get the children to subtract one from a given number.

⑤ Add ten

Learning objective	To be able to add ten to any two-digit number.
Resources	• 100 square overlay • elephant cards (3 colours) • marker dots (4th colour) • number cards 1–100 • drawstring bag
Preparation	Choose a single-digit number. Place the number card on the overlay above the appropriate number. Put the remaining single-digit numbers in the bag.

▶ Ask a child to put the appropriate number of elephant cards on the board, covering the numbers. Mark the last elephant with a dot.

How many elephants will there be if I add ten more elephants?

▶ Count out ten more elephants and count on to find the new number. Mark the new last elephant with a dot and note its number. Show the children that *adding ten* is the same as *counting on ten* or moving *forward ten* on the 100 square overlay.

How many elephants are there now?
What is ten more than x?

▶ Ask how many elephants there would be if you added ten more. Find out by counting out ten more elephants and mark the new last elephant with a dot.

Can anyone see a pattern coming?

▶ Repeat the activity (using monkey cards if necessary) until the children can see the pattern created by adding ten. Remove the elephants marked with a dot. Notice that all the numbers end with the *same digit* and form a column on the square.

▶ Choose another single-digit number from the bag and repeat the activity. After a few times put all the numbers in the bag and add ten to the chosen number without using the elephants or marking the number square as a reference.

Extension 1

▶ Ask the children to subtract ten from a given number.

Extension 2

▶ Use the two-digit number cards to make sub-totals of 30, 40, 50, etc. Arrange beforehand that the cards you put on the board will give additions within the range of the children's ability.

Unit 7: Special numbers

1 Sports Day

Learning objective	To understand why even and odd numbers are so called.
Resources	• monkey cards • elephant cards
Preparation	Put four elephants and five monkey cards at random on the board.

▶ Explain that the elephants and monkeys are going to have a Sports Day and they want to be sure that the teams for different games are fair (i.e. the same number on each side).

How can we make sure there is the same number on each side?

▶ You want the children to suggest pairing the monkeys and elephants together. Build up a team of each animal – one monkey, one elephant, two monkeys, two elephants, etc. Each time you make a pair ask how many animals can play a game altogether – 2, 4, etc. and write these numbers next to the teams.

▶ When you reach the ninth animal you will have one *odd* one left over. Discuss how eight animals lets you have equal teams but with nine there is one left over. Write 8 and 9 on the board. Give 8 a tick and 9 a cross.

▶ Put two more elephants and one more monkey on the board. Arrange all the animals at random and pick teams again in the same way. Discuss and record the result as before (i.e. put 12 in your list and give it a tick).

▶ Finally remove two elephants and three monkeys. Repeat the activity. Record the result – 7 with a cross and 6 with a tick. Ask if anyone can see a pattern in the results.

If there are two animals – one monkey and one elephant – could we make equal teams?
Suppose there are two monkeys and one elephant. How many animals would that be altogether?
Could we make equal teams?

▶ If necessary use the cards to show what would happen. Record the results in your list. You want the children to spot that even numbers of animals give equal (even) teams, but odd numbers of animals means there is one odd one left over. Explain that even numbers split into two equal parts (share by two exactly) and odd numbers always have one left over if you try to share them in two.

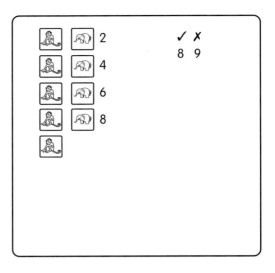

2 Odd and even pairs

Learning objective	To be able to identify any odd or even number up to 100.
Resources	• number cards 1–100
Preparation	The first time the game is played use the number cards 1–20 only. As the children's ability improves, use up to approximately 50 cards, ensuring there are even numbers of even cards and of odd cards.

▶ Place the cards at random, face down on the board. Turn over two cards. If both cards are odd or both cards are even, remove them from the board and turn over two more cards. If you turn over one even number and one odd number turn them back and ask a child to have a go at finding a pair. If the child is successful remove the cards from the board and let him/her have another go. If the child fails to find a pair then another child has a go. If you have a child with a particularly good memory you may wish to restrict the children to no more than two tries each!

Extension

▶ Ask the children to find pairs of odd and even numbers alternately.

Unit 7: Special numbers

③ Doubles

Learning objective	To revise the meaning of 'double' and the doubles to ten. To discover the doubles of 6 to 10.
Resources	• elephant cards • coloured squares • 2 sets of digit cards • optional: addition and multiplication sign cards, equals sign card
Preparation	Sort out seven elephant cards, six different and one a duplicate of one of the six.

▶ Put the six different elephant cards at random on the board. Put the seventh next to them.

Can anyone find his double?
Why did you chose that one? (Because it is the same.)
A double of something means it is, or it looks the same.

▶ Put three squares in a 3 x 1 rectangle.

Can someone make the double of this shape?

▶ Explain that the double gives you three more squares.

I had three squares, how many do I have when I double the number of squares?
How could I write that as a number sentence?

▶ Write, or use the number and addition sign cards, to put 3 + 3 = 6 next to the squares. If the children are familiar with the concept and notation ask them to write the multiplication sentence too.

▶ Set five squares out as they appear on a dice. Ask someone to make the double/double the number of squares. Ask for the number sentence(s). Repeat the activity until you have all the doubles of 1 to 5 on the board. (Remove the elephants to give more room.) Rearrange them and their number sentences to read from 1 + 1 = 2 to 5 + 5 = 10.

▶ Repeat the activity to find the doubles of 6, 7, 8, 9 and 10.

Extension

▶ Discuss what happens if you halve the even numbers. If the children are familiar with halves as fractions $\frac{1}{2}$ discuss what happens if you halve the odd numbers. When is it reasonable to talk about *half* and when is it not – sharing cakes and sharing people.

④ Double fives

Learning objective	To be able to double any of the fives or tens up to 50.
Resources	• marker dots of assorted colours
Preparation	Put five green dots in a row.

How many dots do we need to double the number of dots?

▶ Ask a child to put five blue dots on the board to extend the row to ten.

How many dots do we have now?

▶ Write the addition or multiplication sentence for the result under the dots.

▶ Repeat the activity using ten and then fifteen dots.

Can anyone see a pattern?

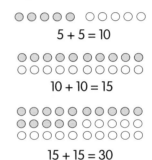

▶ Show them a whole row of ten doubles to give you another whole row of ten. Half a row of ten (five) doubles up to give you a complete row of ten (ten).

What will happen if we double twenty?

▶ Remove the dots on the board so far and lay out twenty dots of the same colour in two rows of ten.

We have two whole rows of ten, so if we double them we will get four whole rows of ten, which makes ...?

▶ Write down the number sentence.

What about twenty-five?

▶ Put twenty-five dots on the board. (You will have to use a second colour for the five.) Explain that doubling two whole rows and one half row will give four whole rows and one whole row, i.e. five whole rows: 50.

▶ Continue (without using the dots, if possible) to find the doubles of 30, 35, 40, 45 and 50.

Extension

▶ Examine and discuss the halves of the multiples of ten up to 100.

23

Unit 8: Number bonds

① Number pairs for twenty

Learning objective	To learn the number pairs for twenty
Resources	• coloured squares of two colours • word cards 'ten', 'twenty' • number cards 0–20 • digit cards 0–10 and an extra 5 and 10

▶ Revise the number pairs for ten. Put the word card 'ten' on the board and ask the children to make the appropriate pairs with the digit cards. Arrange them in order beneath the word 'ten'. Put the word card 'twenty' on the board and the number card 11 beneath it.

▶ Place eleven squares on the board in a row of ten and one more beneath them.

How many do we need to get from 11 to 20?

▶ Ask a child to put enough squares of the second colour on the board to make the pattern up to twenty.

How many did we need? (Nine)

▶ Write 9 next to the 11 in your list under 'twenty'.

▶ Repeat the activity until you have all the number pairs from 11 + 9 to 15 + 5.

Who can see a connection between the number pairs for ten and the number pairs we have made for twenty?

▶ Point out that the pairs are the same except the pairs for twenty have a 1 (i.e. one ten) in front of one number. Discuss why this is (twenty is *one ten* more than ten).

▶ Complete the list from 10 + 10 to 20 + 0 and remove all other cards from the board. Ask questions which involve using these number pairs such as:

There are 20 seats on a bus. 16 are occupied – how many are empty?

Number pairs for twenty

10 + 10 = 20	20 + 0 = 20
11 + 9 = 20	19 + 1 = 20
12 + 8 = 20	18 + 2 = 20
13 + 7 = 20	17 + 3 = 20
14 + 6 = 20	16 + 4 = 20
15 + 5 = 20	

② More number pairs for twenty

Learning objective	To learn the remaining number pairs for twenty (from 0 + 20 to 10 + 10).
Resources	• coloured squares of two colours • number words 'ten', 'twenty' • number cards 1–20 • digit cards 0–10

▶ This activity consolidates the work in activity 1. Approach this in the same way as the previous activity.

Place one square on the board.

How many squares do we need to get from 1 to 20?

▶ Ask a child to put enough squares of the second colour on the board to make two rows of ten.

How many did we need? (Nineteen)

▶ Write 19 next to the 1 in your list under 'twenty'.

▶ Repeat the activity until you have all the number pairs from 1–5.

Who can see a connection between the number pairs for ten and the number pairs we have made for twenty?

▶ Point out that the pairs are the same except the pairs for twenty have a 1 (i.e. one ten) in front of one number. Discuss why this is (twenty is *one ten* more than ten). Ask the children to predict the pairs for 6 to 10.

▶ Complete the list from 1 + 19 to 10 + 10 and 0 + 20. Remove all other cards from the board. Ask questions which involve using these number pairs such as:

There are twenty chocolates in a box. If I eat four of them how many are left?

Unit 8: Number bonds

③ Number pairs with 'teens'

Learning objective	To consolidate the number pairs for a 'teen' (any number from 11–19) and a single-digit number.
Resources	• 2 sets of digit cards • 3 addition sign cards

▶ Building on the knowledge of number pairs below ten, a teen and a single digit number can easily be added together. Ensure all the additions you give the children are within their current knowledge of number pairs.

▶ Write 13 + 2 = on the board.

What does this mean? How can we do it?

▶ You could count on, but encourage the use of number pairs.

Can anyone see a number pair they know?

▶ Make a further prompt by asking:

What does 13 really mean? (How many tens and how many units?)

▶ Use the number cards to put 10 + 3 + 2 beneath the original sum.

Can anyone see a number pair they know now?

▶ The children should recognise 3 + 2 as 5. Change the 3 + 2 cards for a 5 and ask the children the answer to the original sum.

▶ Repeat the activity with other 'teens' and single digits.

Extension

▶ Ask the children to add a single digit number to any two-digit number,
e.g. 32 + 3 becomes 30 + 2 + 3 = 30 + 5 = 35.

④ What do I need?

Learning objective	To become familiar with the number pairs learnt so far.
Resources	• word cards 'two', 'three', 'four', 'five', 'ten' and 'twenty' • marker dots in two colours
Preparation	Chose a number (e.g. 5) and place its word card and the appropriate number of dots (in an easily countable pattern) at the top of the board.

▶ Put some marker dots (e.g. three) on the board.

How many do I need to make five?

▶ Put, or let a child put, the appropriate number of dots (in the second colour) on the board. Write the addition sentence on the board.

▶ Repeat the activity for all the number pairs for your chosen number. Repeat it again with another chosen number.

⑤ Number pairs and addition

Learning objective	To use known number pairs to help with addition.
Resources	• number cards 1–9, 11–19
Preparation	Separate the single-digit and the two-digit numbers. Shuffle the cards and place them in two piles face down on the table.

▶ Place the top cards from each pile on the board (e.g. 6 and 12). Ask the children to add the two numbers together. Encourage them to use number pairs (6 + 2 = 8) to get the answer. For additions such as 17 + 8 use the number pair 17 + 3 = 20, so 17 + 8 becomes 17 + 3 + 5 or 20 + 5.

▶ When you have used all the cards, shuffle them again and repeat the activity.

Extension

▶ Use the single-digit cards 1–9 (from the digit cards and the number cards) and all the two-digit cards.

Unit 9: Subtraction

① How many left?

Learning objective	To introduce subtraction as the inverse of addition.
Resources	• coloured squares • word cards 'one' to 'twenty', 'take away', 'subtract', 'minus', 'equals' • subtraction sign card • optional: equals sign card
Preparation	Place the word cards at random at the bottom of the board. Put eighteen squares in a pattern of 5, 5, 5 and 3 on the board.

How many squares are there?

How many would there be if I take one away? **(17)**

▶ Show the children by removing one square.

▶ Put the square back.

How many would there be if I take three away? **(15)**

▶ Show the children by removing the three squares.

Can anyone use the word cards to make up a sentence about what we have just done?

▶ Put the three squares back. Prompt by asking:

How many did we start with? What did we do? How many did we take away?

▶ Show the children the sentence by repeating the subtraction, but this time just separate off the three squares. Use the word cards to say *eighteen take away three equals fifteen*.

How could we write that as a number sentence?

▶ Introduce the subtraction sign card. Write the number sentence beneath the words. Explain that *minus* and *subtract* mean the same as *take away*.

▶ Show the children you can check the answer by recombining the squares.

If we look at the fifteen squares and put the three back, how many do we have? **(Eighteen! The number we started with.)**

▶ Ask for and write the *addition* sentence on the board beneath the subtraction.

▶ Repeat, using other subtractions. Use the word cards 'take away', 'minus' and 'subtract' and ask the children to complete word sentence and number sentences (subtraction and addition) for each.

② What's the difference?

Learning objective	To be able to perform simple subtractions in the form of finding differences.
Resources	• 2 face cards • coloured squares
Preparation	Draw part of a number line (from 5–8) at the top of the board. Put the face cards on the board. Write *6 years old* above one face and *7 years old* above the other.

What is the difference in the ages of these two children? What is the difference between them?

▶ Explain or ask the children to explain why it is one year. Use the number line to show the space between the ages is one. Show them you can either count on, use number pairs or *take away*.

▶ Arrange two groups of squares, seven squares and six squares.

What is the difference between these two sets of squares?

▶ Explain or ask the children to explain why it is one square or one.

▶ Arrange two more groups of squares and ask for their difference. Write: *The difference between ☐ and ☐ is ☐*. Fill in the boxes with the help of the children. Ask if anyone can think of a number sentence (subtraction).

▶ Repeat the activity, finding differences between sets of squares and writing the number sentence for each. Check each answer by either counting on (addition) or performing a *take away* (subtraction).

Extension

▶ Use the number line overlay and write on it a section of the number line between 0 and 100. Ask the children to tell you the difference between any two numbers you choose.

Unit 9: Subtraction

③ Sorting elephants

Learning objective	To practise number pairs to twenty by subtraction.
Resources	• 20 elephant cards of assorted sizes and colours • word cards to match the number of elephants • 2 sets of digit cards 0–10

▶ Put up to 20 elephant cards on the board, depending on which number pairs you want to practise. Let the children count how many elephants there are. Put the word card for your chosen number above them.

How many blue elephants are there?

▶ Put the appropriate word card on the board.

So how many elephants aren't blue?

▶ Put the appropriate word card on the board.

How many small elephants are there?

▶ Put the appropriate word card on the board.

So how many elephants aren't small?

▶ Put the appropriate word card on the board.

▶ Ask as many questions as you can about the elephants, asking first for the children to identify a set of elephants and then to give you the number of remaining elephants.

▶ When you first play this game you may wish to separate off the 'positive' set of elephants, but try to play without doing this as you do not want the children to count the remaining elephants.

Note: Number cards could be used instead of word cards.

Extension

▶ Ask questions with two criteria. For example:

How many large red elephants are there?
How many elephants are either red or blue?

④ How many more?

Learning objective	To be able to find the difference between two two-digit numbers by counting on or back and recognising the use of number pairs in larger numbers.
Resources	• 100 square overlay • 6 marker dots • Put dots on two numbers in the first row (e.g. 8 and 5).

How many more is 8 than 5?
What is the difference between these numbers? **(Three)**
Why?

▶ Accept any reasonable strategy to find the difference – subtraction, counting on, counting back or number pairs. Ask if anyone had a different way of finding the difference (two methods for each difference is sufficient).

▶ Now put dots on two numbers in the same columns as before but on a different row (e.g. 38 and 35).

What is the difference between these numbers?
(Three)
Why?

1	2	3	4	●	6	7	●	9	10
11	12	13	14	15	16	17	18	19	20
21	22	23	24	25	26	27	28	29	30
31	32	33	34	●	36	37	●	39	40
41	42	43	44	45	46	47	48	49	50
51	52	53	54	55	56	57	58	59	60
61	62	63	64	65	66	67	68	69	70
71	72	73	74	75	76	77	78	79	80
81	82	83	84	85	86	87	88	89	90
91	92	93	94	95	96	97	98	99	100

▶ Explain that the difference is the same because the space between the numbers is the same. Show them you can get the answer by counting on or back and, because they are in the same row and the number in the tens column doesn't change, they can use number pairs to find the difference.

▶ Repeat with two similar numbers (e.g. 78 and 75).

▶ Now repeat the whole activity starting with a different pair of numbers in the first row. As the children's grasp of the idea improves start with a pair of numbers not in the first row. (Always place the dots in the same row. Subtractions which go 'over the break' of a ten are more complex.)

Extension

▶ Place the marker dots on different rows and show how the difference can be found by:
   – counting on to the next ten, counting how many whole tens there are and counting on to the required number. For example: 72 – 56

$$+ 4 \text{ to } 60$$
$$+ 10 \text{ to } 70$$
$$+ 2 \text{ to } 72$$
$$4 + 10 + 2 = 16$$
The difference is 16.

   – counting back in the same way.

Unit 10: Addition 2

1) Larger first

Learning objective	To be able to find a total of two numbers by counting on by the smaller number.
Resources	• coloured marker dots • addition sign card • equals sign card • number cards 1–100

▶ Remind the children that addition is commutative by recording the sums 4 + 3 = 7 and 3 + 4 = 7 on the board.

▶ Talk about how the positions of the 4 and the 3 in the sum make no difference to the answer.

▶ Now use the numbers and addition and equals sign cards to make another addition sum on the board. Place the larger number first, e.g. 17 + 5 =. With the class, work out the answer by putting five marker dots on the board and using these to help you count on from seventeen. Repeat the activity a few times with children choosing how many dots to put on the board and working out the answers by counting on.

▶ Now put up a sum such as 2 + 25 =. The children will probably wish to put 25 dots on the board. Let them do the sum that way and then ask if anyone can see a quicker way to reach the answer. Point out it would have been better to 'put 25 in your head' and count on two dots.

▶ Repeat the activity with the sums having a mixture of the larger number first or second until the children recognise it is usually easier to count on by the lower number.

2) Add five

Learning objective	To be able to add five to any two-digit number.
Resources	• 100 square overlay • elephant cards • marker dots • number cards 1–100 • drawstring bag
Preparation	Choose a single-digit number. Place the number on the overlay above the appropriate number. Put the remaining single-digit numbers in the bag.

▶ Approach this activity in the same way as 'Add ten' (Unit 6 Activity 5).

▶ As a class, read out the numbers you have marked. Count and move your hand in a rhythmical way to emphasise the pattern. You want the children to notice that all the numbers marked end with one of two digits. They will also notice the numbers form two columns on the number square. Check that the children understand that each number covered is five greater than the previous one.

▶ Choose another number from the bag and repeat the activity. After a few times put all the numbers in the bag and add five to the chosen number without using the elephants as a reference. (You may wish to mark the pairs of single-digit numbers with different coloured dots, e.g. 1 and 6, blue; 2 and 7, yellow; 3 and 8, red; 4 and 9, green; 5 and 0, blank.)

Extension

▶ Ask the children to subtract five from a given number.

3) Add two

Learning objective	To be able to add two to any two-digit number.
Resources	• 100 square overlay • elephant cards • marker dots • number cards 1–100 • drawstring bag
Preparation	Choose a single-digit number. Place the number on the overlay above the appropriate number. Put the remaining single-digit numbers in the bag.

▶ Approach this activity in the same way as 'Add ten' (Unit 6 Activity 5).

▶ As a class, read out the numbers you have covered. Notice that you are either reading *even numbers* or *odd numbers*. Notice the digits the numbers end with. The children will also notice the numbers form columns on the number square. Check the children understand that each number covered is two greater than the previous one.

▶ Choose another number from the bag and repeat the activity. After a few times put all the numbers in the bag and add two to the chosen number without using the elephants or the number square as a reference.

Extension 1

▶ Get the children to subtract two from a given number.

Extension 2

▶ Get the children to add or subtract three to/from a given number by adding/subtracting two and then one more.

Unit 10: Addition 2

④ Bridging 10

Learning objective	To be able to add two single-digit numbers with a total greater than ten.
Resources	• number line overlay • number cards 1–20 • marker dots (2 colours)
Preparation	Draw a second number line under the first with space between them for you to put two rows of marker dots. Lay out the number cards on the number lines 1–10 and 11–20.

▶ Write the sum 8 + 6 = on the board. Ask for some ways of finding the answer. The children will probably suggest counting on, in which case remind them it is more efficient to start with the 8 and count on 6.

▶ Leave the *addition sentence* on the board and beneath it write 8 + 2 =.

Who can tell me the answer to this?

▶ If the children know the *number pairs* for ten they should be able to answer immediately. Remind them that knowing number pairs means you can give the answer to some additions without having to work them out.

Can anyone see how knowing this (8 + 2 = 10), can help me to find an answer to this: 8 + 6 = ?

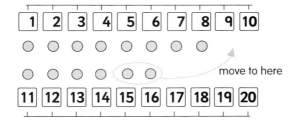

▶ Lay out eight marker dots of one colour beneath the 1 to 8 on the number line. Put six dots of the other colour under these (matching up with 11 to 16).

We know 8 + 2 = 10, so I'm going to use two of these dots to make the eight up to ten.

▶ Slide the last two dots on the second row to the end of the first row.

**How many are left here? (Point to the second row.) (Four) So we have ten (Indicate the ten on the top row.) and four. (Indicate the remaining four.)
How many altogether? (Fourteen) (Show the children that the dots now stop at fourteen and there are no gaps.)**

▶ Start again. On the board write: 7 + 5 = .

Who can tell me a quick way to find the answer?

▶ Put the dots on the board again – a row of seven and a row of five. You want the children to partition the numbers to make one up to ten. They could either say:

Seven and three makes ten which leaves two from the five. So the answer is ten add two – twelve.

▶ Or they may see it as:

Five and five is ten which leaves two from the seven. So the answer is ten and two – twelve.

▶ Both ways are equally acceptable. Demonstrate the addition by moving the dots so everyone can see what is happening.

▶ Repeat the activity with other additions of single-digit numbers totalling eleven to twenty.

Extension

▶ Extend the activity to adding a single-digit number to any two-digit number, i.e. bridge any ten.

⑤ Making tens

Learning objective	To be able to add a set of numbers by combining pairs of numbers to make ten.
Resources	• 2 sets of digit cards 0–9 • word cards 'add', 'altogether', 'total'
Preparation	Place the digit cards at random on the board.

I want to find the total of all these numbers. I want to find how many they add up to altogether. I want to add them all up.

▶ Put the words on the board.

How can we make it easier for ourselves?

▶ Notice that seven and three (for example) come to ten. Put them together on one side of the board. Ask for another pair which makes ten. Put the pairs under each other, in a column down the board. When all the pairs have been made you can count in tens to find the total.

Extension

▶ Include some extra digits so that not all the digit cards pair to make a ten. You will then have to add on the 'extra' ones.

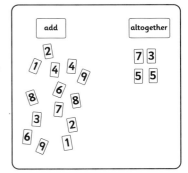

29

Unit 11: Multiplication 1

① Repeated addition

Learning objective	To understand multiplication as repeated addition.
Resources	• elephant cards • word cards 'sets of', 'times', 'altogether' • picture cards 1–5, 8–9, 11–12, 14, 16–19

▶ Put an elephant on the board and explain that he wants to buy some socks.

How many socks will he need? (Four)

▶ Draw four socks next to the elephant and write *4* next to the socks.

▶ Put two more elephants on the board and ask how many socks they will need. Draw four socks for each of them and write 4 + 4 = 8 next to them.

▶ Repeat with three and four elephants (you need not draw the socks each time). Now put ten elephants on the board and start to repeat the process. When you are writing out the addition complain that it is going to be a lot of writing. Review what you have written before.

Here I wrote 4 once, here I wrote 4 twice, here I wrote 4 three times, etc.
How many times will I need to write 4 for these elephants?

▶ Work out the answer by counting in tens (10 right front feet, 10 left front feet, etc.) Use the word cards to repeat the multiplication sentence.

Ten times four equals forty.
Ten sets of four equals ...

▶ Finally introduce the notation × for multiplication and show how it saves a lot of writing. Choose a picture card, e.g. 3 parrots, and work out how many socks they would need (three sets of two.) Repeat the activity with the other animal picture cards.

② Multiplication is commutative

Learning objective	To understand multiplication is commutative, and to learn the words multiply and multiplication.
Resources	• coloured squares
Preparation	Make a 4 × 3 rectangle of twelve coloured squares on the board.

▶ Ask the children for a number sentence about the rectangle. Accept an addition sentence or a multiplication sentence. Ask for any others they can think of.

▶ You want to end up with 4 × 3 = 12 and 3 × 4 = 12. Write them underneath each other (removing any addition sentences you may have). Read the sentences to the children. Ask them for other words they know for *times (sets of)*. Introduce the words *multiply by*, *multiplied by* and *multiplication*. Write them on the board.

What do you notice about the two number sentences?

▶ You want the children to notice the figures have been written in a different order. Explain they both can mean *four sets/lots of three* or *three sets/lots of four*. Each time you have twelve squares. Show them the groups of three or four by indicating a column or row on the rectangle.

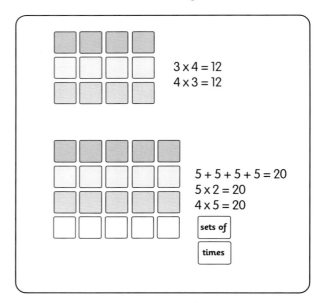

▶ Make other rectangles on the board. Ask a child to give you a multiplication sentence about each rectangle. Write the multiplication sentence on the board. Ask another child to give you the other sentence and write it on the board. Discuss how each sentence has considered the rectangle as sets of rows and columns.

Unit 11: Multiplication 1

③ Making squares

Learning objective	To learn the multiplication pairs for the squares to 5 × 5.
Resources	• elephant and monkey cards

▶ Give a child four elephant cards and ask him/her to make a square with them on the board.

▶ Ask another child to make a different sized square (not larger than 5 × 5) with some more elephant cards. Continue until the children have made the five possible squares from 1 × 1 to 5 × 5. The squares will be randomly placed on the board, so ask the children how you could tidy up the board (i.e. put them in order from 1 × 1 to 5 × 5).

▶ Start with the 5 × 5 square and, with the help of the children, write the appropriate multiplication sentence under each square. Discuss what would happen if you turn the number sentences round (they stay the same).

④ Making rectangles

Learning objective	To learn the multiplication pairs up to 5 × 5.
Resources	• coloured squares
Preparation	Make a 2 × 8 rectangle out of squares at the top of the board.

What shape have I made?
Give me a multiplication sentence for this rectangle.

▶ Write 2 × 8 = 16 beneath the rectangle.

What is another multiplication sentence for this rectangle?

▶ Write 8 × 2 = 16.

How many squares did I use? Can anyone make another rectangle with 16 squares?

▶ They will be able to make the same rectangle but orientated the other way, i.e. vertically instead of horizontally. Show the children that this is the same rectangle as before and has the same multiplication sentences.

▶ You want the children to make the 4 × 4 and 1 × 16 rectangles. (The 1 × 16 rectangle has to be placed diagonally to fit on the board.) Ask the children for the multiplication sentences for these rectangles. Use words like:

4 by 4   *4 sets of / lots of 4*
4 times 4   *4 multiplied by 4*

▶ Try to make other rectangles with 16 squares by systematically working through 1 ×, 2 ×, 3 ×, etc. See if any of the children can tell you when you have tried all the possibilities.

▶ Repeat the activity using 12 squares, but this time be logical from the beginning – start with 1 ×, 2 ×, etc.

Extension

▶ Let the children make all the rectangles and squares (squares are just special rectangles) up to 5 × 5. Encourage them to find the rectangles in a logical order.

▶ Give them a multiplication square to complete and ask them to colour duplicate totals (i.e. colour all the 8s blue, all the 12s green, etc.) Ask the children to leave the diagonal (including the 4) blank. Discuss the pattern formed by the numbers.

⑤ Elephant families

Learning objective	To practise multiplication pairs up to 5 × 5.
Resources	• elephant cards • word card 'sets of'

▶ Arrange a number of elephants on the board, laying them out in a rectangle. For example you might choose three red, three blue, three yellow and three green elephants.

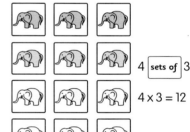

How can we describe this family? (Three elephants in four different colours, 4 sets of 3. Use the word card.)

▶ Write 4 × 3 (or 3 × 4) on the board. Ask how many elephants there are altogether and write the answer to the multiplication sentence.

▶ Repeat the activity with different elephant families, of varying colours and sizes. Arrange them in arrays (rectangles) so that the multiplication facts can be easily seen. Keep all the arrays within the range of 5 × 5.

Unit 12: Fractions

In this Unit you should only use the number sentences if the children are familiar with the operation notation, otherwise omit them.

① Monkey teams

Learning objective	To understand what is meant by *one half*.
Resources	• monkey cards

▶ Put six monkeys on the board.

How many monkeys are there? (Six)
I want to split the group of monkeys in half to make teams for a game.

▶ Write the word *half* next to the monkeys.

How many teams will there be? (Two)

▶ Divide the group into two unequal parts (4 and 2) by drawing a line.

I have divided the group into two teams – have I cut it in half? (No.) For the two parts to be halves they must be equal in size.

▶ Remove the incorrect line.

How many monkeys will each half have?

▶ Divide the group in half by drawing a line through the middle.

If we divide something in half we get two equal parts.

▶ Repeat the activity by dividing other groups of monkeys in half.

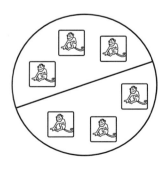

half

one half of six equals three

$\frac{1}{2}$ of 6 = 3

6 ÷ 2 = 3

Extension

▶ Put eight monkeys on the board and split the group into quarters.

② How many halves?

Learning objective	To understand that two halves equal one whole one.
Resources	• elephant cards
Preparation	Make up a group of eight elephants. Have 2 large and 2 small blue elephants and 2 large and 2 small red elephants. Arrange the cards in a rectangle on the board.

▶ Discuss the sizes and colours of the group.

▶ Remind the children that *fraction* just means part of something. If we cut or share something into *equal parts* we can give the parts a name.

▶ Draw a line to split the group into adults and children. Talk about the number of parts (two) and the number of elephants in each part (four), i.e. you have two equal parts.

What fraction of the elephants are adults (large elephants)?
What fraction of the elephants are children (small elephants)?

▶ Discuss how two halves of the group make up one whole group.

What fraction of the elephants is red?
What fraction of the elephants is blue?

▶ Discuss how the group can be split into two halves in different ways, but still two halves of the group make up one whole group.

▶ Discuss things that the children can think of that can be split into halves. Talk about how many pieces you get and that they must be the same size.

Extention

▶ Repeat the activity, but split the group into quarters and discuss how four quarters equal one whole one.

③ Writing fractions

Learning objective	To understand how to write *half* and *quarter* as numbers
Resources	• monkey cards

▶ Put a red and a blue monkey on the board.

How many monkeys are red? (One)
How many monkeys altogether? (Two)
What fraction of the monkeys are red? (Half)

Unit 12: Fractions

- Write *half* and $\frac{1}{2}$ on the board. Explain that *half* means one piece out of two, so we write it as 1 out of 2.

  How many halves make a whole one? (Two halves)

- Say *a half add a half makes one whole one* as you write $\frac{1}{2} + \frac{1}{2} = 1$ on the board.

- Repeat the activity with one red monkey and three blue monkeys to explain the notation for a quarter.

④ Halves and quarters

Learning objective	To partition a number of objects into two halves and then into four quarters.
Resources	• marker dots • 4 face cards: 2 girls and 2 boys • optional: number cards, division sign and equals sign cards

- Place eight dots (in an easily countable pattern) on the board next to a boy face card.

  How many chocolates does Richard have? (Eight)
  Here comes Emma.

- Put a girl on the board.

  Richard's going to share his chocolates, half for him and half for Emma. How many groups of chocolates will there be? (Two)
  How many chocolates will each child have? (Four)

- Share the chocolates between the children.

  Has he shared the chocolates fairly? Has he made two halves? Why do you think yes/no? (Equally sized sets)
  If we divide something equally in two, what fraction do we make?

- Write the word *half* next to the chocolates.

  How many chocolates does each person have? (Four)
  What is one half of eight?

- Say *one half of eight equals four* and write $\frac{1}{2}$ of 8 = 4 under the word *half*.

  How many did we share/divide by?
  How could we write what we have done as a division sentence?

- Write or use the cards for: 8 ÷ 2 = 4.

- Continue finding half of even numbers of dots.

Extension 1

- Discuss what would happen if there were five or another odd number of dots.

Extension 2

- Repeat the activity but share the chocolates between four children to find quarters.

⑤ Equivalent fractions

Learning objective	To understand that two quarters equal one half.
Resources	• assorted coloured squares

Who can make me a square that is half green?

- Assuming the square is made of four coloured squares, any arrangement of colours will do, providing two of the coloured squares are green. Leave the square on the board and copy the arrangement of green squares next to the large square. Write *one half* above the green squares.

Who can make me a square that is one quarter green?

- Again with a square of four coloured squares, any arrangement of squares will do, providing only one of them is green.

Who can change this square so that it is two quarters green?

- Leave the square on the board and copy the arrangement of green squares next to the large square. Write *two quarters* above the green squares.

What do you notice?

- You want the children to notice that one half and two quarters are both made up of two small squares. Discuss how one half and two quarters are the same thing.

33

Unit 13: Number patterns 2

1) Counting in threes

Learning objective	To be able to count on in threes.
Resources	• 100 square overlay • marker dots

▶ Start at zero and ask the children to tell you which number is three more than zero (Three). Mark the 3 with a dot. Continue counting on three up to 99.

▶ With the class, read aloud the numbers you have marked. To help to get a rhythm to the counting, the children should clap as you point to the numbers which are not marked: clap, clap, three, clap, clap, six, etc.

Note: Number cards 1–100 could be used instead of marker dots.

2) Add three

Learning objective	To be able to add three to any two-digit number.
Resources	• 100 square overlay • marker dots • number cards 1–100

▶ Put a dot on any number (e.g. 34) and ask the children to tell you the number that is one more. Cover that number with its number card (35). Point to 34 again and ask for the number which is two more. Cover 36 with its number card. Now ask for three more than 34. Point out that they know what two more is, so they just have to go on one more from that. Cover 37 with its number card.

▶ Put the dot on another number (e.g. 75).

What is two more than 75?

▶ Cover 77 with its card.

What is three more than 75?

▶ Repeat the activity a few more times, asking the question in two stages. Include numbers which cross into the next ten. Then ask for three more without asking for two more first. Remind the children to think *2 more and 1 more than that*.

Extension 1

▶ Use the same activity to subtract three from any two-digit number.

Extension 2

▶ Repeat the activity but count on or back two and two more to be able to add and subtract four.

3) Multiples of 2, 5 and 10

Learning objective	To be able to identify the multiples of 2, 5 and 10.
Resources	• 100 square overlay • number cards for the chosen times table

▶ Do this activity for one times table at a time. Either by counting on, or by saying the table, find and cover the appropriate numbers on the 100 number square to about 50.

▶ Look at the patterns of the numbers:
 – × 2: all numbers end with 2, 4, 6, 8 or 0.
 – × 5: all numbers end with 5 or 0. 5 × odd numbers gives 5.
 – × 10: all numbers end with 0 and start with the multiplying number.

▶ Ask the children to predict the multiples from 50 to 100. (Times tables don't stop at 10 ×.) Ask questions about the numbers.

Is 24 in the 2 xtable?

Is 33 in the 5 × table?

Is 90 in the 10 × table?

If I have 12 sweets can I share them fairly between two people?

Can I make 36p by using only 5p pieces?

Note: The questions only ask if the numbers are multiples of a given number, you are not interested in how many times 10 goes into 90 or 2 goes into 12. The answer to a question in maths does not always have to be a number.

Unit 13: Number patterns 2

④ Repeating patterns

Learning objective	To be able to identify a repeating pattern and predict an element in it.
Resources	• elephant cards
Preparation	Make a line of a repeating pattern of 4 elephants: one large red elephant, one small blue elephant, etc.

Can anyone see a pattern? What do I need to put next?

▶ With the help of the children continue the pattern with a few more elephants. Get the children to tell you it is a *repeating pattern* and that there are two elephants to each repeat. Notice the 1st, 3rd, 5th, etc. elephants are identical, as are the 2nd, 4th, 6th, etc. elephants (*odd* and *even* positions). *Predict* what is needed for the *n*th position.

▶ Repeat the activity with another simple repeating pattern.

Extension

▶ Make more complex patterns using the marker dots.

⑤ Growing patterns

Learning objective	To be able to identify a growing pattern and predict an element in it.
Resources	• marker dots
Preparation	Make a simple growing pattern out of dots. Show the first three groups.

What will the next group look like?
How many dots in the first/second/third group?
What is happening to get to the next group?/What is the difference in the number of dots in each group?
Predict how many dots will be needed for the next group.

▶ Make the next group in the pattern and see if the prediction was correct.

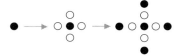

⑥ Designer!

Learning objective	To randomly generate a repeating pattern and be able to reproduce it.
Resources	• marker dots of assorted colours • digit cards 1–6 • drawstring bag
Preparation	Put the digit cards into the drawstring bag.

▶ Take two cards from the bag. Make a repeating pattern of two colours based on those numbers, e.g. if you select 4 and 3 you make a pattern of four red, three blue, four red, three blue, etc. When you reach the end of the row continue onto the next row. This pattern would look like this (assuming 12 dots make one row).

▶ Alternatively when you reach the end of a row start the new row with a different colour.

Note: Dice could be used instead of cards inside a bag.

Extension 1

▶ Let the children make their own patterns on squared paper. (The rows don't have to be twelve squares long.)

Extension 2

▶ Discuss why some patterns make simple stripes down the page. (The repeats fit exactly into one row, i.e. the length of the row is a multiple of the pattern repeat.)

Unit 14: Addition 3

1) Add twenty

Learning objective	To be able to add twenty to any two-digit number.
Resources	• 100 square overlay • marker dots, number cards 1–100

▶ Put a dot where zero would be and put the number card 20 on twenty.

If I start at zero and add twenty, where do I get to? (Twenty)
How many complete rows do we move along to get from zero to twenty? (Two)
So adding twenty is the same as moving two rows.
What would 10 add 20 be?

▶ Mark 10 with a dot and show how you land on 30 if you move two rows.

What has happened to the units digit? (Nothing)
What has happened to the tens digit? (It's gone up by two.)

▶ Repeat the addition with other numbers (e.g. 26 + 20).

▶ Choose any two-digit number and ask the children to add twenty to it.

Extension

▶ Subtract 20 by counting back two rows.

▶ Show the children how they can add/subtract 19 or 21 to any number by increasing/decreasing the tens by two and adjusting the units by one as appropriate.

2) Adding three numbers

Learning objective	To be able to add three single-digit numbers in an efficient way.
Resources	• addition/subtraction template overlay • word card 'altogether' and cards for numbers • monkey cards
Preparation	Draw a line to join the top two rings.

▶ Put some monkeys in each of the three rings. Point to the first ring.

How many monkeys are there here? (e.g. three)

▶ Put the number card 3 beneath the objects. Repeat for the other two rings.

3 + 5 + 7 =

How many monkeys do we have altogether?

▶ Put the word card 'altogether' on the board.

How can we find out?

▶ The children may suggest counting or adding. Use whichever methods are available to them depending on how competent they are with number pairs, doubles, etc. If they suggest counting ask for another way to find out. You want them to suggest *adding* or using *number pairs*.

▶ Possible strategies are to:
   – put the highest number 'in your head' and count on
   – use known number pairs to add 'automatically' and count on any not yet known
   – recognise number pairs of ten and start with these.

▶ Write, or use number cards, to put the addition sentence below the rings. Explain, or ask a child to explain, the strategy used in doing the addition. For example: 3 + 5 + 7 =
7 and 3 make 10, 10 and 5 is 15.

▶ If you write the explanation down *do not* write:
7 + 3 = 10 + 5 = 15! (If you look at the first and last part of the 'sentence' you would have written 10 = 15!) Instead, split the calculation into separate sentences: 7 + 3 = 10 and 10 + 5 = 15.

3) Add three consecutive numbers

Learning objective	To be able to add three consecutive numbers with ease.
Resources	• coloured squares
Preparation	Chose three *consecutive* numbers below ten. Write them on the board and place the appropriate number of squares next to each number, making a neat 'staircase'.

I want to add these three numbers together.
I want to know how many squares there are here.
Look at the pattern.
What happens if I move this square to here?

▶ Move the end square of the largest number to the end of the row for the smallest number.

What shape do we get?

Unit 14: Addition 3

How many rows does it have?

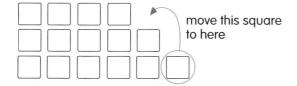

► Explain that you have a rectangle with three rows, each row being as long as the middle number. Move the square back and repeat the movement if some children haven't 'seen' what has happened.

► So you want to know what three lots of *middle number* comes to. Find this by multiplication or doubling and then adding the number again.

Note: Marker dots could be used instead of coloured squares.

Extension

► Find the sum of larger consecutive numbers according to the ability of the children. Try numbers such as 29, 30, 31.

4 Twos, fives and tens

Learning objective	To be able to add multiple amounts of twos, fives and tens.
Resources	• marker dots in three different colours
Preparation	Put a key at the top of the board explaining that the first colour is worth two, the second colour is worth five and the third colour is worth ten.

► Scatter the dots over the board and explain you want to know the total value or *sum* of all the dots.

We could just add on the value of each dot as we come to it (2 + 5 + 2 + 10 + 5, etc.).
That is quite difficult – can anyone think of a better way?

► You want the children to suggest sorting the dots into their colours, adding each colour separately and then combining the three totals.

► Sort all the 'twos' and count (or multiply) 2, 4, 6, 8, etc. Write the total next to the dots.

Sort all the 'fives' and count (or multiply) 5, 10, 15, 20, etc. Write the total next to the dots.

Sort all the 'tens' and count (or multiply) 10, 20, 30, 40, etc. Write the total next to the dots.

► Finally, add the three totals.

5 Number squares

Learning objective	To improve addition skills.
Resources	• number cards 1–9
Preparation	Place the cards in random order on a 3 × 3 grid on the board.

```
          16
    1  4  6  ⇒ 11
    5  7  2  ⇒ 14
    3  8  9  ⇒ 20
    ⇓  ⇓  ⇓
    9  19 17    17
```

► Ask the children to find the three horizontal, three vertical and two diagonal totals. Use different strategies to find the totals:
 – number pairs
 – making tens
 – counting on
 – finding doubles and near doubles, and noticing consecutive numbers may be useful with larger squares or different numbers.

Extension 1

► Choose nine digits at random from more than one set of number cards.

Extension 2

► Make a 4 × 4 grid of numbers.

Extension 3

► Challenge the children to find a magic 3 × 3 square, where all the totals come to 15. Use only the digits 1–9. One solution is:

```
    6  1  8
    7  5  3
    2  9  4
```

Unit 15: Multiplication 2

① Lay the table

Learning objective	To become familiar with multiplication facts up to 5 x 4.
Resources	• marker dots of assorted colours • picture cards 1–5 • drawstring bag
Preparation	Divide the board into up to four regions. Complete it as shown in the picture. Put the dots into the bag. Shuffle the picture cards and put them face down on the table.

▶ Adapt this game according to the ability of the children. Explain that you run a cafe and you have four different sets of cutlery. Take a dot from the bag and turn over a picture card (e.g. a blue marker dot and the 2 lions card).

The lions are having their lunch and they need the blue set of cutlery.

▶ Put the lions in the blue segment (e.g. knife, fork, spoon). Ask questions about the situation.

How many lions are having their lunch?
How many knives/forks/spoons will I need to lay on the table?
How many pieces of cutlery are there altogether?

▶ Talk about this as *x* sets of *y* or as *multiple addition*.

▶ Put the 2 lions picture card back on the table and let a child choose the next customers and their cutlery set.

② Ten times table

Learning objective	To learn the ten times table.
Resources	• six elephant cards • marker dots • number cards 10, 20, 30, 40, 50, 60, 70, 80, 90, 100

▶ Put the elephants in a line down the left-hand side of the board. Explain that the elephants go to a baker's shop and buy some buns. Ask a child to give the first elephant ten buns (marker dots). Repeat with the other five elephants.

How many buns did the baker sell to the first elephant?

▶ Put 10 next to his buns.

How many buns had the baker sold after the second elephant went shopping?

▶ Put 20 next to his buns.

▶ Continue with the other elephants. Read out the results.

One set of ten makes ten. Two sets of ten makes twenty, etc.

1	2	3	4	5	6	7	8	9	●
11	12	13	14	15	16	17	18	19	●
21	22	23	24	25	26	27	28	29	●
31	32	33	34	35	36	37	38	39	●
41	42	43	44	45	46	47	48	49	●
51	52	53	54	55	56	57	58	59	●
61	62	63	64	65	66	67	68	69	70
71	72	73	74	75	76	77	78	79	80
81	82	83	84	85	86	87	88	89	90
91	92	93	94	95	96	97	98	99	100

▶ Ask the class to say it with you.

Which number will we reach if we count on ten more?

▶ Lay out all the multiples of ten to 100 at the bottom of the board. Read out the numbers together.

▶ Clear the board and write *one set of ten makes ten*.

How could we write that in symbols? What do we write for one? Which symbol means set of or sets of? etc.

▶ As the children tell you the symbols, write them under the appropriate words. Repeat the 'table' as before and write it in symbols as you speak. Continue up to 10 × 10. (Make sure you align the units as you write each line.) Notice the patterns in the table – all the 'answers' end in zero and they all start with the number of tens you were counting.

Extension

▶ Give each child a copy of the ten times table to take home and learn.

Unit 15: Multiplication 2

③ Five times table

Learning objective	To learn the five times table.
Resources	• elephant cards • marker dots • number cards 5, 10, 15, 20, etc.

Either: Approach this in the same way as Activity 2 'Ten times table'
Or: Write out the five times table (keeping units aligned) without the 'answers'. Go up to 10×5.

What does $1 \times 5 =$ mean? (one lot of five, five once, etc.)
How many do I have if I've got one lot of five?

▶ Fill in the answer in the table. If the children aren't sure show them with five marker dots or squares.

Which other answers do we know?

▶ They should be able to fill in $10 \times$ if they have learnt the ten times table. They may remember $5 \times$ from 'Making squares' (Unit 11 Activity 3) and $1 \times$, $2 \times$, $3 \times$, $4 \times$ and $5 \times$ from 'Making rectangles' (Unit 11 Activity 4). Discover any they do not know by making the appropriate rectangles with marker dots or squares (or by giving buns to elephants).

Extension

▶ Give each child a copy of the five times table to take home and learn.

④ Two times table

Learning objective	To learn the two times table.
Resources	• elephant cards • marker dots • number cards 2, 4, 6, 8, 10, 12, 14, 16, 18, 20

Either: Approach this in the same way as Activity 2 'Ten times table'
Or: Use the alternative method used for the five times table. Fill in $1 \times$, $10 \times$ and $5 \times$ first. Then move on to $2 \times$ (squares), $3 \times$ and $4 \times$ (rectangles). Finally, complete the remainder of the table.

⑤ Ten times

Learning objective	To be able to multiply any one- or two-digit number by ten.
Resources	• digit cards • marker dots
Preparation	Draw tens and units columns on the right-hand side of the board.

▶ Put two dots on the board. Write $10 \times 2 =$.

What is ten times two? What are ten lots of two?

▶ Make up ten pairs of dots and count them (2, 4, 6, etc.) Write the answer into the multiplication sentence.

▶ Repeat for three more single digits, forgoing the counting out of dots when the children seem able to give the answer to the calculation without them.

▶ Write *2* in the units column.

$10 \times 2 = 20$
$10 \times 3 = 30$
$10 \times 4 = 40$

T	U
	2
2	0
	3
3	0
	4
4	0

What is ten times two?

▶ When the children give you the answer write it in the columns. Repeat for the other numbers you chose. Look at the results. Discuss what has happened to the each number when it was multiplied by ten. Multiplying by ten gives us more. The digits moved one column to make them bigger. Instead of meaning two units the 2 now means two tens – we show there are no units by putting in a zero.

Extension 1

▶ Repeat the activity for 1. Show, by using dots, that multiplying by ten changes *1* into *10*. Discuss how this relates to the names of the columns. Ask what will happen if we multiply 10 by 10. Show it by using dots. Write the results in the columns. Discuss how the 1 and the 0 of 10 have both moved and we have written an extra 0 to show there are no units.

▶ Write $10 \times 12 =$ on the board and ask the children what they think the answer is. Use the digit cards to put 12 in the columns. Show the children that moving the digits in the same way as before gives the result 120. Ask them to multiply any two-digit number you choose by ten. Show them the answer can be found by moving the digits and including an extra zero as before.

Extension 2

▶ Ask the children to multiply a three-digit number by ten.

Extension 3

▶ Ask the children to multiply a one- or two-digit number by one hundred.

Unit 16: Division

① Sharing

Learning objective	To understand division as sharing.
Resources	• face cards • marker dots • word cards 'shared', 'between', 'equals' and a few numbers including 'eight', 'four', 'two' • number cards 1–20 • division sign card • equals sign card
Preparation	Draw a circle on the board as shown below and put the faces on the board. You can give them names if you wish. Arrange eight dots in the centre of the board in two rows of four. Place the word cards at random on the bottom of the board.

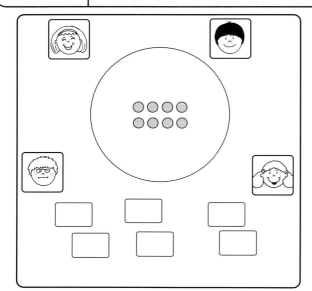

The children have bought eight sweets. They are going to share them. Can anyone tell me how many will they get each?

▶ Collect a range of answers, each time asking the child *why?* they think that is the answer.

▶ Show the children that if you share the sweets – one for Tim, one for Rani, one for Ben, etc., they end up with two each. Ask a child to make a word sentence about what you have just done (eight shared between four equals two). Use the number, division and equals signs cards to make the equivalent number sentence. Explain the sign is called a division sign and explain it as *something (•) shared by (–) something else (•)*.

Now let's look at what happens with twelve sweets.

▶ Arrange the twelve dots in three squares of four, just slightly separated.

How many do you think they will get each this time?

▶ Some children may be able to tell you *3* straightaway from the arrangement of the dots. Perform the sharing, one for you, one for you, etc. and make up the number sentence.

▶ Repeat the activity with other simple divisions, sharing between two, three, four, five or six people. Each time use the cards or write the appropriate division sentence.

② Repeated subtraction

Learning objective	To understand division as repeated subtraction.
Resources	• monkey cards • 15 yellow marker dots • number cards 1–20 • optional: division sign card, equals sign card
Preparation	Put fifteen oranges (marker dots) on the board. You could place them in a tree.

▶ Explain that the monkeys like to eat the oranges and they come to pick them from the tree.

How many oranges are there?

▶ Write *15* near the oranges.

The first monkey is going to pick three oranges.

▶ Put a monkey on the board and give him three of the oranges.

Here comes another monkey. He's going to pick three oranges.

▶ Put the second monkey on the board and give him three oranges.

▶ Continue until all the oranges are picked from the tree.

How many oranges did we start with? (Fifteen)
How many monkeys picked three oranges? (Five)
So how many times can you take three away from fifteen? (Five)

Unit 16: Division

There are five lots of three in fifteen.

▶ Demonstrate by indicating the groups of oranges.

We say 'three goes into fifteen five times'.

▶ Write it on the board.

How else could we describe what we have just done?

▶ Use the word and division and equals sign cards or write the responses on the board.

▶ You want the children to tell you:

Five lots of three makes fifteen.
Fifteen divided by five equals three.
Fifteen shared between five equals three.
5 × 3 = 15
15 ÷ 5 = 3

▶ Repeat the activity performing other divisions by repeated subtraction. Discuss the ways of describing the activity to consolidate the vocabulary and write the relevant number sentences for each one.

③ Arrays

Learning objective	To be able to give two related division sentences.
Resources	• marker dots
Preparation	Make an array of three rows of four dots.

▶ Explain you are going to do some baking and your bun tin looks like this.

○ ○ ○ ○
○ ○ ○ ○
○ ○ ○ ○

How many rows are there? How many columns are there? How many cakes can I make?

▶ Ask a child to tell you a multiplication sentence about this array and write it on the board.

I want to share these twelve cakes amongst three people. How many will they get each?

▶ Demonstrate that there are three rows, one row per person, so each person gets four cakes. Draw a line between each row to show how they separate out. Ask a child for the division sentence and write it on the board: 12 ÷ 3 = 4.

▶ Rub out the lines.

Now I want to share these twelve cakes amongst four people. How many will they get each?

▶ Demonstrate that there are four columns, one column per person, so each person gets three cakes. Draw a line between each column to show how they separate out. Ask a child for the division sentence and write it on the board under the first division sentence: 12 ÷ 4 = 3.

▶ Discuss how if we know one sentence we can automatically write down the other.

▶ Repeat the activity by dividing up other arrays of numbers. Use real examples, such as cake boxes, egg boxes, etc.

④ Pirates

Learning objective	To practise division.
Resources	• marker dots • 10 face cards • word cards 'sixty', 'ten', 'five', 'four', 'three', 'two', 'one'
Preparation	Put 60 marker dots (fifteen of each colour), and 10 face cards on the board.

Some pirates have gone to a secret island and dug up their hoard of treasure. They are going to share it out. How many jewels do you think there are altogether?

▶ Let the children estimate and then tell them there are sixty and put the word on the board.

▶ Say there are ten pirates and ask the children to help you write a division sentence to show how the jewels will be shared out. Write 60 ÷ 10 = on the board. Ask the children to estimate how many jewels each pirate will get.

▶ Ask a child (or two) to perform the actual sharing. Count the jewels and complete the division sentence.

The greedy pirate leader thinks he wants more treasure than only six jewels so he tells half the pirates to set sail in a boat to a far-off land. How many is half the pirates?

▶ Remove five faces from the board.

How many jewels do you think each pirate will get now?

▶ Discuss why they should get more treasure than before. Ask two more children to share the treasure out again. Write the division sentence on the board.

▶ Repeat the process for four, three, two and finally one pirate, each time getting the pirate leader to get rid of his unwanted colleagues. Write the division sentence on the board each time. You could finish the story by saying that the last pirate to leave had taken the last boat, so although the pirate leader ends up with all the treasure, he can't do anything with it because he's stuck on the island alone.

Unit 17: Addition and subtraction

1 Cover your tracks

Learning objective	To practise adding and subtracting two, five and ten from any two-digit number.
Resources	• 100 square overlay • coloured squares
Preparation	The first time you play this game you should ask the questions yourself and ask the children to show you which square to cover. When the children understand the rules you could split the class into two teams and have one asking the questions and the other covering the numbers. The object of the game is to cover as many numbers as possible. A number is covered when it is landed on.

▶ Pick a starting number at random and cover the number with a square. You then ask the children to add or subtract two, five or ten. Cover the number you land on. There are two rules:

1. You may not ask the same question twice in succession (i.e. you cannot continually ask to add two in order to cover half the board.)
2. You may not ask a question which takes you to a number already covered.

Extension

▶ Include a system of 'losing a life' if a question is asked which breaks either of the rules. When all the lives are lost that team's turn ends.

2 Falling leaves

Learning objective	To practise addition/subtraction skills.
Resources	• number cards (amount and numbers according to the abilities of the children).
Preparation	Draw a tree on the board and place the numbers on the branches like leaves.

▶ Ask the children an addition. The answer is one of the leaves of the tree. When they give you the correct answer remove the leaf from the tree. Repeat until all the leaves have fallen.

▶ You could adapt this into a competition between two teams. Draw two trees. Either you ask questions to alternate teams or the team members have to make up and answer their own questions.

Extension

▶ Ask questions which involve all of the arithmetic operations, using as varied a vocabulary as possible, including doubling and halving.

3 Number detective

Learning objective	To improve addition/subtraction skills.
Resources	• number cards 1–9
Preparation	Make a number square with four of the digits 1–9 and calculate the totals. Remove some of the digits from the square and some of the totals. Ensure that the square can be completed. Each solution should make it possible to complete another line.

▶ Ask the children to be number detectives to find out what the square originally looked like. Here are two possible starting grids.

	5	
7	3	
	8	5

	6	10
	1	
		14

4 Fill the blanks

Learning objective	To improve addition/subtraction skills.
Resources	• digit cards 0–9 • 2 sets of addition sign cards • 2 equals sign cards

▶ Use the cards to make up an addition sum on the board, but leave one of the numbers out (e.g. 16 + _ = 24). Ask a child to put in the missing number.

▶ Repeat the activity with other additions. As a variation you could ask the children to make up the sums. They must be able to provide the correct answer.

Extension

▶ Play the game using all of the arithmetic operations cards.

Unit 17: Addition and subtraction

(5) Cops and robbers

Learning objective	To improve addition/subtraction skills using numbers up to 100.
Resources	• 100 square overlay • 2 marker dots (2 colours) • 1 coloured square • number cards 1–24 • drawstring bag
Preparation	Put the number cards in the bag. You may wish to play a simpler version and use only numbers 1–10.

The 50–50 gang has just robbed a bank in One Hundred Square.

▶ Put the robbers' counter on 100.

They are making their getaway to their hideout on Fifty Street.

▶ Put the coloured square on 50.

The police, in First Avenue police station, are trying to catch them at their hideout.

▶ Put the police counter on 1.

▶ Divide the class into cops and robbers. They move their counters by drawing a number from the bag. (The number is then discarded.) If it is an *even* number they *add* it to the number of the square they are on. If it is an *odd* number they *subtract* it from the number of the square they are on.

▶ If any calculation would take them past 1 or beyond 100 they stop on the 1 or 100 and the actual answer does not need to be found.

▶ The first group to reach 50 is the winner. They do not have to land exactly on 50.

▶ If the counters land on the same square, the cops win.

▶ When all the numbers are used you can either find out who is closer to the hideout by finding the difference between the players' numbers and fifty, or put the numbers back in the bag and carry on.

(6) The power of doubling

Learning objective	To practise multiplying by two and to illustrate how quickly repeated doubling of a number produces a very large number.
Resources	• 10 x 10 grid • 1 marker dot • coloured squares • 2 sets of digit cards 0–9

Jim and his parents were trying to decide how much pocket money he should get each week. He made a suggestion to his parents. He said, 'Next week give me 1p for my pocket money, the following week double it to 2p, the following week double it again to 4p, and so on. At the end of the year whatever you are giving me then, I'll keep as my amount of pocket money until I'm old enough to earn money for myself.'

The parents agreed (especially as 1p and 2p seemed very small amounts of money). Would you agree to that suggestion? (Why?)

Let's see what happened. How many weeks are there in a year? Let's mark where 52 is on the grid.

How much money did Jim get in the first week? (1p)

▶ Use the digit cards to record 1p and mark off the week with a coloured square.

How much did he get in the second week? (2p)

▶ Mark the week and record the amount.

▶ Continue the activity with the children performing the doubling for as long as their ability allows. By the time you reach week 12, the idea that the amount is becoming very large is probably beginning to be obvious (and Jim was on to a good thing!).

Week 1	1 p
Week 2	2 p
Week 3	4 p
Week 4	8 p
Week 5	1 6 p
Week 6	3 2 p
Week 7	6 4 p
Week 8	£ 1. 2 8
Week 9	£ 2. 5 6
Week 10	£ 5. 1 2
Week 11	£ 1 0. 2 4
Week 12	£ 2 0. 4 8

▶ Ask the children to guess how much Jim would be getting by the end of the year.

▶ If you were to continue up to 52 weeks Jim would be receiving more than £22 million million pounds (£22,000,000,000,000) a week!!!

43

Unit 18: More number problems

This unit includes activities which use all four arithmetic operations. The children may have to choose the appropriate operation, or the activity can be adapted to give practice in using a particular operation that you choose.

1) Good guess!

Learning objective	To practise estimating a number of objects.
Resources	• marker dots

▶ With the board turned away from the children put a number of dots at random on the board. Turn the board towards the children and show it to them for a few seconds. Ask them to *estimate* how many dots there are on the board. Keep a record of their suggestions and then count the dots with the children and compare with their estimates.

▶ If there are fewer than seven objects the estimates should be very close.

▶ When you use larger numbers try putting the dots in patterns and see if the estimates improve.

▶ Ask the children to estimate to the nearest ten.

▶ Play the game over several weeks and see if the estimates improve.

▶ Try using a mixture of dots and squares, or ask the children to estimate the number of a particular colour.

2) Rounding

Learning objective	To be able to round a two-digit number to the nearest ten.
Resources	• number line overlay • number cards 1–100 • drawstring bag
Preparation	Draw a number line across the top of the board and spread out the cards 0, 10, 20, 30, 40, ... 100 at equal intervals along it. Put the remaining cards in the bag.

▶ Explain that we don't always need to know a number exactly. Knowing it roughly is sometimes good enough. For example, it may be good enough to know there are about 60 pencils in the tin – we don't need to know there are exactly 63. Ask the children for examples of when a *rough* or *round number* is good enough.

What numbers are we counting in on this number line? (tens)

▶ Ask a child to pick a number from the bag and show it to the rest of the class.

Where does x fit on the number line? Roughly, where should it go?

▶ Say the child picks 47, you want him/her to show you it goes between the 40 and the 50. Ask the class if they agree. Put the number in its approximate position.

▶ Now using the number line on the overlay move the 40 to one end.

Which ten belongs at this (the other) end? (50)

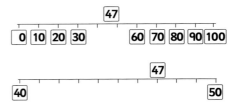

▶ Move the 50 to the appropriate place and count the numbers and marks on the expanded number line: 40, 41, 42, 43, ... 50. Ask a child to put the 47 in the correct place on the expanded line.

Is 47 is closer/nearer to 40 or to 50?

▶ If the children aren't sure mark half-way with a large dividing line.

We can round 47 up to 50. 47 is approximately/nearly equal to 50.

▶ Write *47 equals 50 to the nearest ten* on the board.

▶ Using the same expanded number line ask the children to round 41, 42, 43, etc. to the nearest ten (pick them at random). Discuss what to do with 45, 40 and 50. Explain that:

▶ If the unit digit is 0, 1, 2, 3, or 4 the number is rounded down.

▶ If the unit digit is 5, 6, 7, 8, or 9 the number is rounded up.

▶ Repeat the activity by drawing numbers from the bag and rounding them to the nearest ten. Use the number lines if necessary.

3) Treasure hunt

Learning objective	To use logical and mathematical thinking in order to identify a given two-digit number.
Resources	• 100 square overlay • coloured squares • number cards • drawstring bag
Preparation	Put the number cards in the bag and choose one at random. Do not let the class see which number you have chosen.

Unit 18: And finally

I have picked a number from 1 to 100. It is my treasure and I want you to try and find it. Ask me a mathematical question about the numbers on the 100 square overlay and see if you can find the treasure. I can only answer 'yes' or 'no'.

▶ Give the children examples of questions they might ask. Here are three:

1. Is it larger than 40?
2. Is it in the five times table?
3. Is it in the 2 column?

▶ Ideally you want the children to eliminate as many numbers as possible with their questions (e.g. *Is it odd?* is a 'good' question as it eliminates half the numbers on the board. *Is it between 6 and 8?* is a 'bad' question as it only eliminates 7.) You can discuss these tactics when they are more familiar with the game. Discourage them from asking *Is it x?*

▶ When the children ask a question you cover all the numbers they eliminate with coloured squares so they are left with fewer and fewer to consider.

Suppose you picked 12, if the children asked the 3 questions above, you would answer:
1. No – cover 41 to 100
2. No – cover 5, 10, 15, 20, 25, 30, 35 and 40
3. Yes – cover all remaining numbers except 2, 12, 22 and 32.

▶ Each time check that the children understand why you are covering certain numbers – double negatives can be confusing. With 'good' questions the children can find the treasure with two more questions.

Extension

▶ Encourage the children to count how many questions they used to find the mystery number. Can they use fewer next time?

④ Number trains

Learning objective	To use number pairs (addition and multiplication) in order to solve a puzzle
Resources	• operations cards • 2 or more sets of digit cards 0–9
Preparation	Put the cards and symbols at random on the bottom half of the board. On the top half draw a 'truck' which is big enough to contain two two-digit numbers and an operations card. You could start the train by putting in a random expression made from the cards available.

▶ Draw the next truck and explain the expression it contains must start with the answer to the first truck, i.e. 12. The remainder of the expression must be made from any available cards and the answer must also be able to be made.

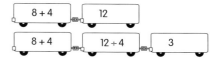

▶ Continue until all the cards are used or no more trucks can be made. Give the last truck (with only one number) a flag to mark it as the guard's van!

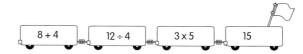

Note: 'Equals' is not mentioned or used in these trains.

⑤ Mixed problems

Learning objective	To be able to identify which operation(s) are needed to be able to solve a problem.
Resources	• marker dots • coloured squares and other picture cards

▶ Make up word problems and use the resources to illustrate what is happening. This will help the children to decide whether they need to add, subtract, multiply or divide in order to find the answer.

Example 1

▶ There are 28 children in a class. 17 are girls. How many are boys?

▶ Count out 17 red dots for the girls (arrange in a easily countable pattern). Count on with blue dots (again arrange in a pattern) until you get 28 children. Count how many boys there are. Discuss the problem as a subtraction.

Example 2

▶ I have three boxes, each containing five pencils. How many pencils do I have altogether?

▶ Count out three groups of five coloured squares. Discuss the problem as a multiple addition or as a multiplication.

Extension

▶ Use more complex problems that need more than one step to reach the answer.

Shape and space

① Resources: marker dots, coloured squares
Use the dots and squares to form rectangles, squares and triangles. Look at the patterns of numbers produced by the number of dots/squares needed to form increasingly larger shapes.

② Resources: coloured squares, marker dots, elephant cards
Use the shapes and cards to make symmetric and asymmetric patterns.

③ Resources: coloured squares
Use the squares to demonstrate nets of cubes and cuboids.

④ Resources: 100 square or 10 × 10 grid overlay, marker dots, coloured squares (to mark positions reached)
Use the overlay to practise giving and following directions, e.g. down, North, South, East, West, right, left, forwards, backwards, etc.

⑤ Resources: 10 × 10 grid overlay, coloured squares
Use the overlay and the squares to mark out a maze. Ask the children to direct you through it.

⑥ Resources: 10 × 10 grid overlay
Draw a shape on the overlay. Find the area of the shape by counting the squares it encloses. Start with simple shapes which follow the grid lines. Gradually introduce shapes which cut squares in half, etc.

Measure

① Resources: marker dots

Use the dots of one colour to represent 10p and ask the children to count how much money is on the board. Similarly represent 5p, 2p or 1p with dots of different colours. When the children can count in ones, twos, fives and tens confidently mix the 'coins' and get the children to sort them into denominations, i.e. 1ps, 2ps, 5ps and 10ps before counting. Get them to practise 'stacking' the 'coins' in groups of 10p, 20p, etc. to make them easier to count.

② Resources: number cards 1–100

Write units of length, mass and capacity next to selected number cards. Ask the children to find the longest, heaviest, fullest, etc.

③ Resources: marker dots

Represent different coins with differently coloured dots. Use the dots to work out amounts of money and change required in simple situations. Ensure the children understand why swapping one 2p for two 1ps etc., is 'fair'.

④ Resources: number cards 1–12, marker dots

Place the numbers as on a clock face to demonstrate times by drawing and rubbing out the hands. Make another clock face with dots instead of numbers next to the first. Draw hour hands on the clock with the numbers, and minute hands on the clock with dots. Show how it takes the minute hand half an hour to cover half the clock. Compare how far the minute and hour hands travel in one hour.

⑤ Resources: number cards 1–12

Place the numbers as on a clock face to demonstrate times by drawing and rubbing out the hands. When the children are familiar with adding halves and quarters you can ask them questions.

What is half and hour and a quarter of an hour?
What time is it half an hour after 3 o'clock?
What time is it half an hour after quarter past 7?

⑥ Resources: number line overlay, number cards 1–100

Place the numbers 0, 10, 20, 30, 40, 50, 60, 70, 80, 90 and 100 along the number line. Mark a point along the line as if it were part of a scale. Explain what the scale is measuring and ask the children for (or tell them) appropriate units. Ask them to read the scale (to the nearest number marked). Make up scales with larger numbers, or scales where the numbers are marked in twos or fives, or at the first and last mark only.

Data handling

① Resources: picture cards 1–20, elephant cards, monkey cards

Use the cards as a basis for sorting. First sort on one criterion, e.g. colour, size, it has legs, it can be eaten, etc. Later you can sort into more sets, e.g. it has two legs, it has four legs or it has more than four legs; or it is red, it is blue, it is green or it is yellow; etc. Alternatively use two criteria with an overlapping Venn diagram, e.g. it is red, it has legs.

② Resources: coloured squares

A simple survey can be conducted in the class. Have no more than five items in the survey and keep the numbers to be recorded smaller than ten. Use the coloured squares to build a block graph. Label both axes carefully and give the graph a title. Ensure the children understand what the squares are counting (i.e. people – not bags of crisps, etc.). Ask questions about the graph.

Which was the most popular?
Which came second?

③ Resources: coloured squares

Make block graphs of heights, ages, weights and volumes of children, objects and liquids. Ask questions about the graphs.

Who is the tallest?
Which weighs the least?